Michel de Certeau
or
Union in Difference

Michel de Certeau

Inigo Text Series: 12

Michel de Certeau
or
Union in Difference

George B. York, II

GRACEWING

First published in 2009

Gracewing
2 Southern Avenue
Leominster
Herefordshire HR6 0QF

and

Inigo Enterprises
Links View
Traps Lane, New Malden
Surrey KT3 4RY

*'The expense is reckoned; the enterprise is begun
It is of God ...'*

All rights reserved. No part of this publication may be reproduced, stored in a retrieval system, or transmitted in any form, or by any means, electronic, mechanical, photocopying, recording or otherwise, without the written permission of the publisher.

© George York 2008

The right of George York to be identified as the author of this work has been asserted in accordance with the Copyright, Designs and Patents Act 1988.

ISBN 978 0 85244 684 3

Typeset by Action Publishing Technology Ltd,
Gloucester GL1 5SR

Contents

Frontispiece: Michel de Certeau — ii
Preface — vii
Foreword — x

Chapter 1: Michel de Certeau: Pilgrim Through
            Language Always — 1
Chapter 2: Who Am I? — 16
Chapter 3: Union in Difference — 47
Chapter 4: Jesus, Believer in Others — 63
Chapter 5: The Wisdom of Uncertainty — 89
Chapter 6: Whither Has Our Guide Brought Us? — 101

Bibliographic notes on *L'étranger ou l'union dans la
   différence* — 106
Books by Michel de Certeau — 108

Truth, however, is to be sought after in a manner proper to the dignity of the human person and their social nature. The inquiry is to be free, carried on with the aid of teaching or instruction, communication and dialogue, in the course of which humans explain to one another the truth they have discovered, or think they have discovered, in order thus to assist one another in the quest for truth ... Moreover, as the truth is discovered, it is by a personal assent that humans are to adhere to it.
– Vatican II, Declaration on Religious Freedom, 3.

... Enriched by the gifts of others ... The result to be sought is unity in diversity.
– Avery Cardinal Dulles, *First Things* (2007).

Preface

In a preface, writers thank those who have helped them on their way. In my case, I wish first to make several remarks about what you are about to read.

I have tried to explain how Michel de Certeau makes it possible for us to think of belief or faith. We will methodically analyse a brief text regarding human belief or trust in others. From that we gain an understanding of faith in the Other, God. Faith begins and ends with the unknown. As believers, we humans are those who, to the extent of our capacity to do so, recognize the limit of our ability to grasp others (and the Other) and therefore discover the sense or direction of faith.

I have written a commentary on a sign of Certeau's spirituality. That sign is his book *L'étranger ou union dans la différence – The Stranger or Union in Difference*.[1] In an age when 'spirituality' is on the lips of many, it helps to clarify what the word means. Fr David L. Fleming notes that a Christian spirituality must offer answers to theoretical questions about being human, about Jesus, and about God. On the other hand, 'spirituality' may be taken more practically, in the manner of Ignatius of Loyola, founder of the Jesuits. Then 'spirituality' refers to 'a way of proceeding', a way of living one's life. One could compare different spiritualities according to how they answer four questions: Who am I? Who are you? Who is God? What shall I do? In the following pages we shall see that what Certeau writes joins both senses of 'spirituality'. Although I will not try to show that it is so, I believe he lays a groundwork for considering any spirituality, not only Christian.

Alan W. Watts once wrote a popular book which he titled *The Wisdom of Insecurity*.[2] He wrote of a spirituality based upon the premise that what we humans need to recognize and go against is any idea and practice driven by a desire to be other than we are. We are insecure, unprotected from the chances of life. His point is well-taken as far as it goes, but its premise is not as fundamental as Certeau's. What Certeau says is that what most differentiates us as human is the recognition of a certain poverty. That recognition liberates us from any illusion that we know more than we do. Thus, in the title to this work, I could have identified Certeau after his way of proceeding, as I have named it, 'The Wisdom of Uncertainty'. Instead, I have identified him after the present and future goal of his way of proceeding: *Union in Difference*.

What I have written could not be without reading. I owe thanks to all those who ever helped me on the way to becoming a reader. Very early in my life my parents, especially my mother, encouraged my interest in books. Next, I believe my early study of writers like Vergil and Cicero were indispensable for learning to read – even if not for learning to write. Next, I thank Fr Michael J. Buckley. I may not have fully understood his approach to texts, but he showed me that I was on the right path as I learned to be a more careful reader.

Here is the place to mention a particular choice concerning spelling. 'Other' and its cousins are important in *The Stranger*. Thus I at times spell them in a way which may seem unusual. When I refer to a second or additional one of anything, I use the word 'another'; for example, 'another discourse'. However when, following the French usage of the Pilgrim, I mean a person; I separate the articles ('the' and 'an') from 'other', I write 'an other' or 'the other'.

A writer cannot be without many others. I wish to thank in particular: Zoë Helene Woolrych York who suffers my reading and reminds me about good writing; Fr Billy Hewett,

Preface

Inigo Enterprises, Oxford, without whose support, encouragement and longtime friendship, this publication would not be. Fr Michael Pastizzo, who got me started on the computer. Compañeros who help keep me informed and curious. Dr Dody H. Donnelly, Graduate Theological Union, Berkeley, CA, for ever encouraging my interest in Certeau, for reading the text and for caring suggestions. Professor Luce Giard, Research Fellow emeritus at the CNRS-EHESS or School of Higher Studies in the Social Sciences, Paris colleague of Certeau, in charge of his literary estate, for reading my interpretation and for her generous help and suggestions. Fr Peter Gallagher, Heythrop College, University of London, for his encouraging evaluation of what I have written; Mr James A. Grout, for friendly dialogues, reading the text and valuable suggestions; and last but not least, Ms Courtney Cowgill, for friendship, reading the text, valuable suggestions and corrections, and putting the text onto CD.

Finally, I must express my deepest thanks and appreciation to The Pilgrim of Language, Michel de Certeau. His voice has been silent now for more than twenty years. But, as so many others attest far better than I, the effect of this unforgettable passer-by remains. He sets a high standard for ordinary belief and thus for ordinary faith. I thank him for having given me the possibility of creating this modest, but for me enlightening, study.

Notes

1. De Certeau, Michel, *L'étranger ou l'union dans la différence*, France, Desclée de Brouwer, 1969. All following references to *L'étranger* are to this edition.
2. Watts, Alan W., *The Wisdom of Insecurity*, New York, Vintage, 1951.

Foreword

George B. York has written an important introduction to the thought of Michel de Certeau (1925-1986). He emphasizes, with great sensitivity, how Certeau, an authority in several disciplines, not least the history of spirituality and the sociology of religion, ultimately presents himself as the opposite of an expert. He shows the reader a humble searcher after truth who is content to acknowledge a genuine Socratic ignorance. The benefit from studying his many works is not because of an enlargement of understanding (although there is much to learn from him) but because of the example he sets in the practice of a particularly generous method of inquiry. An acknowledgement of the poverty of present understanding permits human beings to enter optimistically into dialogue with all that is different from them. There is a strong, justifiable hope of building unity. This harmonization is not the abolition of difference or the imposition of uniformity or sameness. The unity constructed is an expression of a profound belief in others and a confidence that what they have to communicate could change a life. The genius of Certeau, as York's *Michel de Certeau, or Union in Difference* makes eloquently clear, is to combine a deep appreciation of the transformative and truth-tracking power of language and action with a firm belief in the authenticity of many different styles of living and expressions of selfhood.

Michel de Certeau came to fame in France in the aftermath of 'the events' of 1968 with his articles about *la prise de la parole*. It was as if 'the word' or freedom of speech were a kind of contemporary Bastille, the invasion and capture of which signalled a new revolution, comparable to that of 1789. George York shows us how his friendly mentor Certeau evolved towards an understanding of spiritual and intellectual endeavour which was more like 'the capturing of silence'. Before others, and especially before their spiritual achievements, the sincere inquirer must fall silent. This silence is respectful and attentive. Its spirit is generous and self-donating but it also hopes for the gift of enlightenment. The 'believer-in-others' who is silent in this way is peculiarly well-equipped to hear what the other is saying and to construct a harmonious response. Respect for self and a proper honouring of the other do not rule out the sort of silent or 'whispering' dialogue which alters the soul. Such alteration might well be mutual but Certeau envisages a pilgrim whose journey is undertaken in such poverty and humility as not to require proof of such alteration in the other.

York shows how the kind of life-pilgrimage recommended by Certeau has in it the outlines of his personal spirituality. This is a religious life conducted on the margins. The radical alteration in conduct and attitudes which is proposed makes no claim to establish a new centre of things, in the manner of an eighteenth-century revolution. Marginalization is truly embraced. The world tends to detect madness in such a degree of humility. De Certeau's early studies in spirituality drew attention to the special 'madness' of such marginalized sages as Surin, Labadie and even Favre. There is a continuity between these historical works and his later, more hopeful vision of what might be done with self-destructive spiritual impulses. The loss of the self can be fairly cheerfully contemplated within structures of belief which favour 'union in difference'. For Michel de Certeau as for his perceptive interpreter, George B. York, a pilgrimage, or life, is undertaken by embarking on a 'migration through meaning'. These two pilgrims, Certeau and York, are not afraid of silence, but do not shrink either from 'the practice of alterity', that is, from a life unflinchingly shared with the other. This excellent book explains, with admirable economy of expression, how harmony can be constructed from difference. 'Heterology', science of the other, has found a new prophet.

Peter Gallagher, SJ
Heythrop College
University of London

Chapter 1

Michel de Certeau: Pilgrim Through Language Always

One of the boldest, most secret, and most sensitive minds of our time.
— Julia Kristeva

Think of one word we can apply to anything and everything. Daily we meet the surprising, the unexpected, and the enigmatic. What word do we use? If we are wise, a word for others as well as for ourselves. A word we can use in the first place for the man who inspires this study. What word sums him up? He himself praised what it stands for.

French is the mother tongue of Michel de Certeau. In it he wrote an essay, *'Apologie pour la différence'*, 'In Praise of Difference'.[1] So, 'difference' is the word we seek. Our word not only for surprises, for the unexpected, for the enigmatic in ordinary life, but also for anything and anyone. It has to be our word for him – and for a fundamental secret of his mind.

What secrets set apart the life and mind of Certeau? The Italian furniture-maker Maggiolini was famous for creating hidden compartments in his master-crafted furniture. Specialists speak of them as 'secrets' or hidden places. To find them it helps to understand how things are constructed. That's why, in this chapter, we will first look at Certeau's life. We will find depth and nobility. His mind was as broad as it was deep. His nobility was based not on class expectations but rather on not identifying himself with any particular social group – he was very clear that being a Jesuit was a personal engagement not a privileged social role. Then we will look at one paragraph from one of his books. We will see that it must be read as two distinct discourses in two different languages. While the language of each discourse signifies the same thing, neither expresses what is between them. Yet, by the end of the following study, we want to know what that 'between' might be and what secret it might disclose about the Pilgrim.

A different life (1925–1986)

Life for Michel-Jean-Emmanuel de la Barge de Certeau began in Chambery in the ancient region of French Savoie. To the north, Swiss Geneva hides in the grey. To the east, Mont Blanc shines in the Alps. To the south beckons ancient Lyons, home of Certeau's mother. There some of his education took place. Far to the west, on the French coast, modern Bordeaux bustles. It, too, set Certeau apart. In 1600 it was the birthplace of Jean-Joseph Surin. Certeau introduced this surprising seventeenth-century Jesuit to the twentieth century. Certeau's birth and growing up were privileged but privilege did not set him apart in life. What did?

I first met Certeau on a corner on the north side of the University of California, in Berkeley, in 1972; he reminded one of *The Little Prince*, a fable for children about adults by Antoine St Exupéry (ex-ou-pay-ree). Exupéry's little person is a pilgrim from a distant place among the stars, who examines others 'with the most intense seriousness'. Certeau was like that: a person with the seriousness of the pilgrim. François Dosse calls his biography of Certeau, *Le Marcheur Blessé* (*The Wounded Pilgrim*).[2] The first time I met Certeau, he gave me a book he had written. He autographed it: 'Michel ... Pilgrim through languages ... always.' That suggests, and Dosse confirms, that reading languages set Certeau apart. From an early age, he read constantly and widely. To read more he slept less. At boarding school, he found ways to read after 'lights out'. Dosse tells us that a not-too-friendly schoolmate quipped that, 'At home rats are better for devouring books in the attic.'

Reading was not the only thing he did wherever he went. Athos is the name of a mountain in northern Greece. It is a mile high at the tip of a peninsula extending into the northern Aegean Sea. The entire peninsula takes its name from the mountain, Athos. The Holy Mountain is home to numerous monasteries of Orthodox monks. In regard to pilgrims coming to the Holy Mountain, the monks rightly observe that coming there is no different from coming to any other place. What makes one's visit different is what the pilgrim does there.

Pilgrims have always been associated with spirituality, by which I mean a way of proceeding, a manner in being with others. So I see Certeau, the Pilgrim, in terms of the movement of prayer. According to traditions rooted in the Mediterranean world of our Semitic, Greek and Roman past, that movement is summarized in an old Latin formula: *'lectio, meditatio, oratio'*. That was the formula of Certeau's day-to-day life: 'reading, meditation, oration'. Our word 'meditation' means thinking. 'Oration' means communication, oral or written speech, voicing or writing what is in one's mind and heart; its Latin root, *oratio*, also means 'prayer'. Certeau bore his Athos, like a book, with him.

What set the Pilgrim apart as reader, thinker and communicator? His thinking is what the following pages are about. As one can see from his writing, his reading was vast. For example, I recall seeing the Pilgrim in Berkeley, a book in hand. It was in English: Sigmund Freud's *Civilization and its Discontents*. The title states the breadth of the Pilgrim's concerns and the depth of his interests. His reading took him to titles on every aspect of life in society and on the struggle to become fully alive. He never stopped reading. Not long before he died, he recommended *Ars Moriendi*, an old book on 'the art of dying'. He said, 'Good reading'.

Certeau was both teacher and writer. What set him apart was his performance in those roles. He engaged others in the pilgrimage through language. Certeau's wide and deep knowledge let him question and answer. He had a wealth of knowledge in many learned and scientific fields from which to draw answers as well as questions. Depending upon the interests of the persons to whom he was speaking, his questions could point them toward the border between what they knew and what they did not. Such questioning would help them progress on their own pilgrimage through language. An attractive ability not only in reading but also in questioning authority placed the Pilgrim apart as both writer and teacher.

Teachers and writers risk becoming prisoners of authority. 'Authority' refers to the origin of ideas, to speakers or writers whose expressions may be taken as a final word upon what may be said and/or done in response to particular questions. The case of Galileo in the seventeenth century is a classic example of how authority imprisons. What Ptolemy wrote about the Heavens was taken as unquestionable; Galileo knew as we do that what Ptolemy said about heavenly motion is not the way things are. Nevertheless, he and his ideas were confined by Vatican authority which blindly followed that of Ptolemy.

In Certeau, fellow students never ran the authoritarian risk. In the words of someone else who knew him, he had 'a way of standing in the question'.[3] His position in relation to any authority, major or minor, was one of sincere respect, and it was one of questioning. Regardless of how much he did know, he never lost sight of the fundamental limits of all knowledge and so of the need for questions. When others represented opposing views, regarding them with the utmost seriousness, his responses always had something of this sense: 'Yes, you can ask that.' Thus, he restored to 'permission' its existential sense. Whenever mutual faith or trust are involved in a human relationship, questions are necessarily present along with the unknown. Mutual recognition of the unknown is fundamental to all communication which then means each side lets or permits the other to question. Speakers then find themselves returning to themselves with the register of their perception or understanding modified; new paths for thought are opened up. The Pilgrim was such a partner in dialogue making possible, or in a very real sense permitting, an altered relation of one to an other as well as of one to the world.[4]

Through his lectures and seminars students in Europe and

the Americas took note of the questions he asked. During the 1970s Certeau took his questions to both North and South America. He took part in many encounters and seminars in Latin America, Canada and parts of Europe. For a time he spent a portion of each year in Paris, at various faculties of higher study, and another portion at La Jolla at the University of California (1978–84). At La Jolla he was for a time head of the Department of Literature. Following that, in 1984, he was elected to the prestigious School of Higher Studies in the Social Sciences, Paris, conducting studies and preparing further publications.

Following his doctorate in Paris at the Sorbonne (1960), Certeau's work began with a focus on editing publications in spirituality, written texts dealing with ways of vital progress. The Pilgrim's first major publication was an edition of the *Memorial* or *Spiritual Journal* of Pierre Favre.[5] Favre, like Certeau a native of Savoie (but four centuries earlier), was among the first companions of Ignatius of Loyola, founder of the Jesuits. Like Favre, Certeau was always on the move to other towns.

It was during the decade of the 1960s that he published editions of works by Jean-Joseph Surin. For a time between 1632 and 1640 Surin was an exorcist at the Ursaline convent of Loudon, France. After that he was a mental wreck for twenty years (he once jumped out of a high window). He recovered and became finally, a prominent spiritual author, a 'mystic', a seeker of the hidden. Certeau called him 'my guardian' – fitting that a Jesuit had another Jesuit as a mentor.

In 1968, with *La Prise de parole* (*The Capture of Speech*), Certeau spoke of the meaning he saw in the student uprisings throughout France during May and June. Of those days he wrote that 'from the beginning to the end, speech is what has played the decisive role . . . I have lingered on this strange fact . . . believing that it was fundamental and that it engaged the entire structuring of our culture . . .'[6] In the 1970s and 1980s the Pilgrim began a new line of research in contemporary culture, publishing in French, *La Culture au Pluriel* (*Culture in the Plural*) (1974) and *L'Invention du quotidien* (*Inventing the Ordinary*) (1980). He published other important scholarly works, among them: *L'Écriture de l'histoire* (*The Writing of History*) (1975) and *La Fable Mystique* (*The Mystic Fable*) (1982). In the last two works he sets the highest standard for contemporary writing of history and the understanding of 'mysticism'. Other authors esteem his work or oppose it. Either way his questions have to be taken into account.

I once asked Certeau: 'Why do you write the way you do?' He replied, 'It's more interesting that way.' In Latin *'inter est'* means something 'is between'. 'More' is a word favoured by Ignatius of Loyola. Was it just me or was Certeau saying that he wrote the way he did because that way placed 'more between us?' What is certain is that his writing was more interesting. For example, we will meet expressions like 'poverty funds all communication'. Reading that, we will have to ask, How can something (all communication) be funded by the absence of something else (a poverty*)*? Then we can wonder: A lack of what?

While Certeau may be surpassed by others in quantity, he is equal to the best in the quality of his writing. Every word is in place in relation to those placed before and after. Each image evokes familiar experience, perfectly expressing what he had 'seen'. Poetic images sprinkled through erudite works seem autobiographical and at times humorous. He alludes to the sea, upon which he was fond of gazing. Or to labyrinthine archives. An image in one of his books suggests them and the exhaustion resulting from time spent devouring old books. Reading those lines, one hears a hungry researcher: 'How do I get out of here?'

When illness accosted him, he kept working nearly to the end. He died 9 January 1986, in his apartment, 'with an elegance and fortitude born in another century: it was he who comforted his visitors ... and spoke to them of the future'. He was buried from the Church of St Ignatius, Paris, 13 January 1986, well remembered and truly missed by very many in America as well as in Europe.

The Stranger

In 1972, the Pilgrim gave me a copy of a book he had written. It is the book surrounding the paragraph we are about to study. It revisits fundamental questions of the structuring of any culture. He called his book, in French, *L'etranger ou l'union dans la difference*. In English it would be called *The Stranger or Union in Difference*. After this, I refer to it as *The Stranger*. The edition of 1969 is the basis for what follows. In it I have found clues to understanding the Pilgrim's life and mind. In fact I found them in that one paragraph. Here it is in his French, followed by my English.

> En confessant notre incapacité à les saisir, nous confessons déjà, et tout ensemble, leur existence, la nôtre (à laquelle nous sommes renvoyés) et une réciprocité fondamentale entre eux et nous. Dans la mesure où nous acceptons de *ne pas identifier à ce qu'ils peuvent attendre de nous, et à ne pas les identifier aux satisfactions ou aux assurances que nous espérions tirer d'eux*, nous découvrirons le sens de la *pauvreté* qui est le fond de toute communication. Cette pauvreté signifie en effet le désir qui nous lie aux autres et la différence qui nous sépare. C'est la structure même de la foi en Dieu.[7] (Certeau's italics)

That is,

> When we confess our incapacity to know others, we confess simultaneously their existence, our own (to which we are returned) and a fundamental reciprocity between them and us. To the extent we *agree not to identify ourselves with anything they can expect from us and not to identify them with satisfactions or assurances we hope to take from them*, we discover the sense of the *poverty* which funds all communication. This poverty signifies in effect both the desire which unites us to others and the difference which separates us from them. The same is the structure of faith in God. (Certeau's italics)

The paragraph concludes a section of a chapter about two-thirds along the way of *The Stranger*.

Once I had read it I knew it was extraordinary. One way to

see it is as an elegant, modern apologetic for the fundamental traditional teachings of Christianity about faith. I am using 'elegant' as scientists do. When scientists say a theory or explanation is elegant, they mean it explains as adequately as possible what is known without unfounded or awkward qualifications. I use 'apologetic' as theologians do to refer to a reasoned defence of Christianity. There is a second way to see the paragraph as elegant. Because it manifests such things as Certeau's wide and varied knowledge, his careful observation of and sympathy for humanity, and his ability to express all that not only in subtle images but also in a pattern proper to his thought, the paragraph reflects the sun of poetry. Finally, while the paragraph does not and cannot demand agreement, it nonetheless sheds light on the connection among many Christian doctrines.

On My Translation

Most of us have had the experience – perhaps too rarely – of really understanding what was on an other's mind. It does happen, and it can happen with what follows. In an interview shortly before he died, the Pilgrim said, 'Our existence oscillates between the desire to possess and to be changed by others.'[8] Listening and reading are like that; we want both to grasp something from an other and to be changed by it. Noticing what happens when we listen is a useful way to understand what happens when we read. When we listen we bring our own difference or history to what we hear. Listening and reading involve the same risk. Understanding this risk is important for following the meaning of the Pilgrim.

Familiar to us all, the risk we face is found first in everyday conversation. A single word or many words together may evoke in a reader-listener's mind any one or even all of the barriers to listening well. Those barriers have to do with details of what is on one's mind: images, memories, meanings for words, feelings – everything which can distance one from what is on an other's mind here and now. To the extent that we pay more attention to what we bring to what an other is telling us, we risk missing what they bring. Then, what's yours is not mine – even when I use your words to say back to you what you have said. In reading, as in conversation, a question must always be: From the words used, am I getting more what I bring to them or more what their author brings; am I getting more of myself than of an other?

Reading, like listening, means trying to grasp as much as possible what others mean by the words they use, signifying what they mean, which can be quite different from what we believe they mean. Besides an awareness of one's differences and the obstacles they may place in the way of understanding an other's meaning, one can bring other tools to reading. First, mutually agreed meanings. Their source? A dictionary. Using an independent authority, one tries to avoid to the extent possible what all the king's men face: that Humpty Dumpty cannot be put together again. In the case of our paragraph from *The Stranger* the French dictionary used (suggested by Certeau) has been *Robert*. With basic meanings established, a reader can then bring to a text like Certeau's paragraph two other tools. One is an awareness of the matrix or context in which a text is embedded. Our word 'context' literally means 'with the text'. In reading Certeau's paragraph I have tried to keep in mind not only each word but also the rest of *The Stranger* and other of Certeau's writings, a few by him in English. Another tool is whatever awareness one has of the issues and questions raised by the words in a text. Not everything is an obstacle to understanding; to the extent that one has special knowledge, it can be helpful.

Both listening and reading involve translation, regardless of whether a speaker or author uses the same tongue as a receiver. 'Translation' means taking something from one side to another. One professional translator has said that when an author writes in another language, the best one can do is translate the words as though the author wrote in the translator's own language. One is attempting the impossible: making entirely one's own something that is not. Nevertheless, approaching that ideal, we are changed, we learn. What we are about to do begins with taking the Pilgrim's words from his French to our English so that we many give them meaning upon our own mental 'pages'.

A translation can be literal or free, word for word or more like an impression of what a writer has written. My goal has been to be as faithful as I could be to each word of Certeau while remaining mindful of context.

One paragraph, two discourses

Before we begin, we need to take care of a few more necessary preliminary considerations. These will give us an initial map of the way ahead. Is the paragraph one text or discourse or is it two? This may seem a strange question, but looking carefully at the last sentence of the paragraph makes it necessary. The last sentence reads, 'The same is the structure of faith in God.' Thinking about the word 'same', we realize a duality is referred to. For something to be the same as something else, there obviously has to be a something else. The Pilgrim refers not to two structures but to two discourses concerning one structure, neither without the other and neither the same as the other. This fact is fundamental to understanding the paragraph.

Why are the two discourses not the same, that is, what are the two structures about? We know the second structure is of faith in God, so the first has to be of faith in something or someone other than God. Faith or trust is an ordinary human response. Normally, besides speaking of faith in God, we speak of faith in one another. Therefore, it would seem that the first structure must have to do with human faith in others. We will be examining the first structure in some of the pages ahead. It gives us the foundation we need for understanding Christian faith in God. That we will examine in due course.

As Certeau says, our religious questions are at bottom human questions. Or, as theologians of old said, nature is the basis on which Grace builds. Thus, the paragraph first speaks of humans in relation to other humans and, secondly, it speaks of humans in relation to an Other. Now we recognize that the paragraph can be read twice within two different contexts.

A discourse is a verbal treatment of a subject. When we speak of 'subject' here we mean 'I' and 'you', one and other or an Other. The paragraph speaks of two subjects; it begins with 'We' and ends with 'God'. The one paragraph contains two discourses. The first subject of both discourses is human, any human. It is you or I who believe. Each discourse begins with 'We', but one ends not with 'in others' but with 'in God'. Grammatically, 'God' is the object of faith. However, when it comes to others, we do not believe in objects but rather in subjects like ourselves. Thus, one discourse contains two subjects: we ourselves as believers in other subjects and we ourselves as subjects who are believed in by others. The second discourse is different to the extent that its second subject is the Other, God who, Certeau lets us say, is not only a subject in whom we believe but also a subject who believes in or trusts us. The second discourse has to do with very different yet somehow related subjects, 'We' and 'God'.

For the sake of emphasizing the fact that there are two discourses, I will distinguish synonyms for two key words found in the paragraph. The first word is 'confess'. It carries a religious connotation which cannot be in the first discourse which, as we shall see, is philosophical, not theological as is the second discourse. In looking at the first discourse, in place of 'confess', I use 'recognize'. Like 'confess', 'recognize' means a sudden acknowledgment or awareness.

The other word is 'faith', which can carry a theological connotation. In the first discourse I use instead the word 'belief'. In regard to the meaning of both 'belief in' and 'faith in', it will become clear that the Pilgrim allows us to take them in the sense of 'trust in' which includes but is not limited to the idea that an other or Other exists. Belief or faith as I am using them here carry the larger connotation attached to 'trust'.

The fact that there are two different discourses will make it necessary to bring different science or knowledge to each: philosophical to one and theological to the other. Reading the first discourse raises questions to be answered through knowledge of philosophy. Reading the second discourse raises questions to be answered through knowledge of Christian Scripture and tradition. From the earliest times, philosophy and theology have been related. It seems to me they are related as halves of a whole. From this point of view, the Pilgrim's dual discourse answers the question: How can we think about faith as well as about belief?

Language

Certeau described himself as a 'Pilgrim through languages'. What do we mean by 'language'? A bit of history reminds us of one sense of the word. The Knights of St John of Jerusalem were like today's soldier-medics, except they were fighters too. For several centuries before, as well as into, the period after the discovery of the 'New World', from 1309 to 1523 the knights occupied the Greek island and town of Rhodes, off the southwest coast of modern Turkey. Inns in the walled town were named for the languages of the knights living in them. They were called the 'Tongues' of England or of France or Spain or Italy, places where those languages were heard. Our Pilgrim is set apart in that he read and spoke those and other tongues. Thus, 'tongues' is one of the senses he had in mind when he called himself a 'Pilgrim through languages'.

We can distinguish other senses for the word 'language'. It can refer to fields of learning, such as the 'languages' of mathematics, science, philosophy, theology, poetry, love and so on. Then, its meaning is close to 'the point of view' of each of those fields. Finally, 'language' can be given a more exact scientific definition: 'a system of signs used to signify or to give knowledge or to express feelings'. As the Pilgrim observes, language in this sense is ultimately the object of science; without language what could we know? Is it going too far to say that language is all there is between us?

The meaning of language as communication or the expression of knowledge and/or feelings, as our way of knowing, is how the word is used in what follows. As far as the languages (points of view) of the two discourses are concerned, the language of the first is philosophy, of the second, theology.

As we have already noted, a third language – poetry – is implied as well. Certeau is master of all three.

An expressive gap or void

Finally, something the Pilgrim says elsewhere allows us to note a very particular and easily missed fact of the two different discourses. Placed side by side, they are separated by a real gap or absence. That gap is significant, but of what? Of a presence? What can the absent be called?

The importance of the fact of the gap and of the questions about it is suggested by Certeau. In his book, *L'absent de l'histoire* (*The Absent from History*), he tells us the following. In the writings of both the Spanish Carmelite monk John of the Cross (died 1591) and of the French Jesuit Jean-Joseph Surin (died 1665), prose and poetry are two ways of approaching the same thing. John's prose works are commentaries upon his own poems; his prose would not exist without his poetry. In the case of Surin the role of poetry is not so immediately visible; nevertheless it is also true that his prose does not exist without poetry. Certeau says of the two approaches that they 'express by the gap [between them] ... what neither expresses alone'.[9]

In the end, two discourses, side by side, and between them a gap. What then is between them? What does the gap or emptiness between two discourses express which neither discourse expresses by itself? That we must come eventually to answer.

Way to a secret

Long ago when books were large and rather rare, they were copied and recopied by monks who devoted their lives to that work. Pages of such books were often quite large, with very wide margins between text and edges of the pages. Through the ages, those books often acquired comments by readers of the main text. For example, an explanation of a particular word in the margin beside a particular text. Such comments are called 'glosses'. Thus, the study in the following pages of the paragraph by Certeau can be viewed as a long gloss in a margin of *The Stranger*.

The glosses are part of an effort to perhaps discover a secret of Certeau's mind. One seems to exist. Yet the more time I spend with the Pilgrim's writing, the more familiar his ideas seem. What is extraordinary is the elegance of his expression and the many different points of view which he seems able to hold together in a unity. Alas, it is the elegance and unity to which I may be judged unfaithful. However, there will be no possibility of reward without the attempt.

Elsewhere in Certeau's writings, he quotes the French Catholic saint, Thérèse de Lisieux. The Little Flower said, 'I believe because I want to.' I take it that she believes because she chooses to. Given the Other, God, there is another way in which she wants. She lacks the Other. The Other is the singular focus of her desire. As we disclose aspects of Certeau's paragraph, we can bear in mind that we are searching for his help in understanding that desire and its limitation. Therefore, to repeat: How can we think about faith in God? Or, what can an understanding of human belief in others show us about faith in the Other?

Our study is neither theological nor psychological, but rather a careful, critical reading of a twentieth-century French writer's elegant, existential description. As we progress, we are in a kind of dialogue with an important figure. The Pilgrim is our author-guide. A thousand years ago, the Italian poet Dante chose the Roman poet Virgil as his author-guide through his poetic vision of hell and purgatory. At the end of their journey, upon the threshold of paradise, a new vision appears and a different guide replaces Virgil.

The Pilgrim, like Virgil with Dante, takes us – if we 'want' – nearer a place where a different vision is possible, where another Guide may take over, where, as our Guide says, 'A door may be opened upon the known or the unknown, but in such a way that we know in advance neither where nor how'.[10]

Questions

Reading about the Pilgrim, what is the impression you get of the person? What seems to be most different about him?

Translation means putting an other's language (point of view) into my own. Isn't that what reading and listening are about? Looking at your experience, what are the obstacles you meet when you try to translate the speech or writing of an other? What is the risk?

What are the key questions before us regarding Certeau's dual paragraph and its two languages?

Notes

1. *L'etranger*, pp. 179–225.
2. Dosse, François, *Michel de Certeau: Le marcheur blessé*, Paris, La Découverte, 2002. For a short biography one may go to the recently released biographical dictionary *Qui Etait Qui; Dictionairre Biographique Des Francais Disparu Ayant Marque Le Xxeme Siecle (Who Was Who in France in the Twentieth Century)*, France, *Who's Who*, 2005.
3. Thanks to Professor Luce Giard for reporting this observation of an other who knew Certeau.
4. Certeau, 'How is Christianity Thinkable Today?' *Theology Digest*, winter, 1972.
5. Works by Certeau mentioned in my text can be found in the bibliography of his writings in French. For works already in English, see internet reference above.
6. *La Prise de parole*, 32–3.
7. *L'étranger*, p. 169.
8. Pessis-Pasternak, Guitta, 'Le corps e les musiques de l'esprit', *Le Monde Aujourd'hui*, Sunday 19 to Monday 20 January 1986.
9. *L'Absent de l'histoire*, p. 59.
10. *L'étranger*, p. 16.

Chapter 2

Who Am I?

You have to be a philosopher.
   Certeau, to a companion

Once, in her eighties, my mother wondered aloud, 'Have you ever asked yourself, Who am I?' The question came and went in an instant. No chance to answer, no chance to enquire: 'Where did that come from?' We were off on the day-to-day questions of what to have for lunch or what to watch on the television.

Who am I? What am I living for? A question probably everyone asks. Is there an answer? One approach is by the study of philosophy. Like the approach of the natural and 'human' sciences, this way remains forever at the door from the known to the unknown. As soon as one door opens another behind it appears. We have no final answer to the universe and everything and philosophy bakes no bread and has no armies. That may be one reason why the word 'philosophy' evokes interest or scorn. Which it is depends upon one's experience and/or upon what one imagines when one hears the word. Be that as it may, 'philosophy' identifies for us the language of our Guide's first discourse. How does its approach to knowledge of who I am differ from the approach of modern science?

Objects and subjects

A friend says simply, 'Philosophy is a search.' From that point of view, the search ahead is a modest one: to grasp how Certeau allows us to think about belief in others, then about faith in God and finally about what one is living for. Some background on the philosophical context of that thinking may help.

Philosophy is a search for knowledge, a scientific search. I am using the word 'science' in the sense of its Latin origin where *scientia* means knowledge. I use 'modern science' when I mean the theoretically and practically effective way of knowing developed over the last five hundred years. The evolving modern sciences of nature (physics, for one) and of human living (psychology, for example) have enhanced our approach to understanding reality.

Like the modern sciences, philosophy (as well as theology) has disciplined thinking at its core. And, also like the searches of modern science, those of philosophy never end. However, there is an important difference between some philosophy and science. As modern scientists we employ a method or way of arriving at things to be said based upon measurements of objects carved from reality, creating representations of such things as atoms, the unconscious, group habits or culture, and so on. The 'objects' of our thinking stand in for what is in reality and for what happens there. We know our thinking is correct when predictions we make about such objects turn out to be rather the case – splitting atoms discloses sub-atomic particles and analysing obscure contents of one's mind demonstrates how one's past is present.

On the other hand, as subjects, thinking philosophically, we can try as far as possible to think of ourselves as subjects with a relation to other subjects, without the inter-position of theoretical objects. Then we are seeking to understand how Certeau lets us think of ourselves as believing subjects. This will not mean ignoring scientific thinking and its results, but it will mean approaching reality, especially human reality, by thinking in terms of subject relations rather than in terms of objects. We are asking: What do I do when I believe or trust in others?

Relation

A word used from time to time in these pages is 'relation', a most basic experience we as subjects have, it is central to existence. We can note several important things. Every relation is singular. I have one relation to you; you have one relation to me. Your relation and mine are not the same. Although we can speak of them as alike, attributing to them the same characteristics, our differences do not allow my relation to you to be literally the same as yours to me.

No relation can be observed. What is observed and so what can be spoken of is behaviour which makes evident various modalities of one's relation to an other: not only belief and love but also things like doubt and hate. What one thinks and wants, what one says and does at any one time can only partially express (through language, verbal and non-verbal expressions) modalities of one's relation to others. The same is true of 'religion', a term which in its root sense ('bound back') means relation. Religion is any historically and culturally defined relation to God.

We can speak of a relation as having a plurality of particular characteristics, qualities describing me as a subject in relation to an other. Belief, love, rights and responsibilities are some of the 'modalities' of a subject in relation to an other. Modalities are alike in that they express various modes in one's manner in being with others whom I believe, love, respect and so on. Modalities differ according to how one's manner in being with others is communicated. For example, belief is expressed more by words, love more by deeds. Modalities in a single subject are alike in that they are expressions of that one subject. From this point of view my love of an other is more or less a modality of my belief in them.

Furthermore, to the extent that one's loving is Christian, that is, to the extent it is charity, it is like but not the same as the love of a non-Christian. Both are real and true but different. Charity aspired to by Christians is different to the extent that it expresses a standard of care for others which is fundamentally different from other standards human caring may express. Fundamentally, charity is not about need or self-interest (enlightened or otherwise). Similarly, to the extent that one's belief is Christian, that is, to the extent that it is faith, it is like but not the same as the belief or faith of other humans. It has the same structure but expresses a relation of a subject to others which is at times perhaps greatly different from that expressed by other human subjects, for example, the going to death of a Christian martyr is different from the death of a witness to a particular cause.

The difference between love and belief and Christian charity and faith has to do with the 'human difference' of subjects who love or believe in others. All humans can love, not all are Christians. Nonetheless, as modalities of a caring relation to others, Christian faith and charity express human belief and love. Finally, faith and charity, like belief and love, are modalities of each other; they are a blend, a union in difference.

In conclusion, from this point of view, we can differentiate 'relation' from 'relationship'. The difference comes from the fact that every relationship is by definition dual, two-sided, composed of the particular relations of two different persons. Careful reading of any newspaper column or book on relationships confirms this: whatever advice is given ultimately pertains to changes this or that individual can make in modalities of their particular relation to an other, for the sake of what is between them, a relationship of two different individuals.

Experience

'Experience' is a word we have already used and will continue to do so. Everyone knows what it means until they try to say. Here that is what it means, that is, something happens which it is not possible to fully define. The problem is in explanation. A sore thumb due to particular contact with a hammer is not mysterious. To the extent that what happens involves a number of possible causes, definition may not be easy; in some cases it may not be possible. For example, what may an episode of fainting be due to? Something about one's body to be sure, but *what* about it? Obviously, something is always happening, what it means is not always so obvious.

Philosophical styles and their risks

One can identify different styles of philosophical search, seeking to understand experience. One style originated among the ancient Greeks; Aristotle is identified with it. So are Thomas Aquinas in the thirteenth century and Jacques Maritain in the last.

Look at or imagine a tree. Now, forget everything you know about trees and try to focus on that single tree and this fact: the tree is. Just that. It is the business of one style of philosophy to focus much attention there and to ask: How can we think about 'is-ness' or 'being'? The technical term for this approach is metaphysics, literally 'beyond physics', the study of what everything physical presupposes. This style takes a particular way to answering 'Who am I?' It speaks of the 'essence' of humanness and comes to expressions like 'rational animal'. We can call this style of philosophical thinking 'essentialist'. Its method is rather deductive and certain, starting with statements which seem unquestionably true. Then one can try, for example, to find how such statements apply logically in the world of experience. One can think: if humans are rational animals, then you are a rational animal because you are human. However, one has to beware that logic is only as good as its assumptions. What if other animals have a rationality different only in degree from that of humans? What then becomes of our human rational animal? Neuroscience shows us what we do not know about rationality, and primate studies show how close chimpanzees are genetically to being human. A recent headline reads: 'Activists want chimp declared a "person".' We construe corporations as persons, why not other 'animals'?

The business of the style which interests us here is to focus less upon 'being-as-such' and more upon 'existence'. The word existence can be taken in several ways. As we are about to see, Certeau emphasizes two of those: 'being-in-the-world-with-others' and 'being as standing out'.[1] In keeping with the root of the word, 'existent' (standing out from), every being in the world is understood as emerging and continuing to stand out as different from any other, even of its own kind. Even a rose among roses is, as Exupéry's Little Prince would say, 'unique in all the world'. This style focuses on being in that sense and so is called 'existential'. Being with or being in relation to others is where existentialists start their search for understanding the way human subjects are in reality.

A method existential philosophers or 'existentialists' employ is called 'phenomenology', a big word for 'description'. Existential stylists try to describe subjective experience as accurately as words allow. Logical inferences can be replaced by looking carefully at how things emerge or play out. In this way light is thrown upon daily life so we understand it with greater clarity. As we proceed we will be reminded here and there of a few striking remarks of existentialists in the twentieth century, Buber in particular, but also Heidegger, Sartre, and Camus.

An existentialist carefully observes and notes, for example, that human caring, concern for an other's growth, can become resentment. A subject about whom I care can come to seem a burden which I resent more than love. When we think about this we may say, yes, I have seen that happen. Then, with details faithful to recognizable experience, an existentialist who carefully describes events in such cases may thereby throw light not only on why such an event happens but also on how it might be avoided. Recognition born of a differentiated understanding can bring a clearer idea of what may need to be done. Notably in regard to relationships, advice makes use of insights gained from the modern human sciences, especially psychology. Such insights afford descriptive interpretations of human existence which can be easily woven into a existential philosophical view.

What existential stylists have to say often sounds in a strange way familiar. That's because their attention is focused on day-to-day or ordinary life. They seek clues in everyday experience for answering questions like, 'How do I know?' and 'Who am I?' They draw conclusions from what can be carefully observed and from what can be said to be generally true and perhaps quite different from 'what everybody says'. As already implied above, since their focus is upon real subjects, existentialists can easily make use of results derived from studies of human existence using theoretical objects as their lenses. Not all existentialists are interested in the sciences. This is one way Certeau, with his careful attention to discussions among those interested in psychology and psychiatry, set himself apart.

Once we understand the existential style, we can find examples of it in the distant past, when what we mean by scientific objectivity existed to a lesser degree. Written when there was no talk of existential style, the Christian Gospels contain what we can call an existential accent. Later, we will see how the Pilgrim lets us bring existentialism and awareness born of modern psychology to the Gospels.

As readers of thinking about our humanity, we have to bear in mind the fact that no one philosophical style says it all. Certain perennial questions, like 'How do I know what I know', are dealt with in every style. Though one style expresses them differently, it may offer answers which complement the answers of another style. Every style may help shed light on corners of life which another style leaves dark. (This is where the history of philosophical styles can be important.) No one serious style of philosophy is necessarily better than another. The essentialist's 'rational animals' are not denied by existentialists, rather they are made more recognizable as ourselves. Indeed, as might be inferred later in our study, human difference can be said to be very like 'the essence' of our being human. Generally, as the description of existence shows, the business of 'being in the world with others' cannot be without the business of 'being' itself. Awareness of different philosophical styles was another way in which the Pilgrim set himself apart.

Every style has particular risks. For example, the essentialist style risks being overly abstract, loaded with jargon and seeming certainty. Then, perhaps without realizing it, one may think of who we are in a way which tends toward the idea that what is important about humans is no more than their 'souls'. For existential stylists, the risk is to become so taken by one area that sight of other areas is lost. They may clearly see a tree but miss how other things stand out and differ on the mountain.

Following the Pilgrim means asking a question of global importance: What do we do when we believe? Answering that is a way of answering 'Who am I?' Careful attention to the language of the first discourse will give us fundamental answers. They are fundamental because they give a firm position from which to look for answers to many other questions. The answers have to do with epistemology and anthropology, two big words for the study of what (and how) humans know and for the study of what makes them human.

The way ahead

We now begin looking closely at each word of the Pilgrim's paragraph in its philosophical mode. Our objective is to discover or decode as far as we can the secrets built into it. In what is to come, we are trying to listen to the Pilgrim telling us something about who each of us is and, therefore, something about belief and faith. We have our map, the paragraph in *The Stranger*. We will reflect upon each word of the Pilgrim's philosophical description.

In this chapter the path our reflection will follow will be along the words of sentences one, the end of sentence two, and sentence three. In the next chapter we will look at the words in the main portion of the more practical sentence two. With some exceptions, we will look at words in the order in which they occur in the Pilgrim's paragraph. For the reader the main question is: How is what I am reading illuminating Certeau's meaning in his paragraph?

In what follows, when a line of several words is followed

by an ellipsis (...) and appears between quotation marks, it means that those particular words or phases are the focus of the following glosses or comments. Elsewhere an ellipsis will simply mean that some words have been omitted from a quotation. Here to begin are sentence one and parts of sentences two and three from the four sentences of our Guide's paragraph.

> When we recognize our incapacity to know others, we recognize simultaneously their existence, our own (to which we are returned) and a fundamental reciprocity between them and us ... [A] poverty ... funds all communication. This poverty signifies in effect both the desire which unites us to others and the difference which separates us from them ...

What is the Pilgrim telling us? Taking a few words at a time, we will build up a fuller picture of what Certeau has elegantly sketched in his dual paragraph.

'When ...'
So begins the first discourse. It refers to a very specific moment of experience with others which inaugurates a particular movement. The movement begins with a particular recognition. It is a moment when we may or may not choose to recognize something. Some human limitation like fear may prevent us; the moment may escape us. Fortunately, the invitation to recognition never leaves us alone for long; recognition is always possible.

'We ...'
In *The Stranger,* 'We' refers to a particular human group. Certeau writes *The Stranger* as one Christian to an other. 'We' means 'We Christians'. But that is where the second discourse begins. Elsewhere in *The Stranger*, the Pilgrim writes that our religious questions are in reality, human questions. What needs to be understood first of all is what can be said of all humans, regardless of the terms of the differentiating characteristics of their particular religion or relation to the Other.

The Pilgrim writes not only as a Christian but also as a human and so, in the first discourse, 'We' refers globally to 'We humans'.

In speaking first of humanity, Certeau is respecting the ancient and necessary relation between philosophical and theological languages. Speaking theologically is not possible without at least one underlying philosophical language. (Even an assembly of unexamined ideas is a sort of philosophical style, increasing the risk of, as they say, 'garbage in, garbage out'.) Like modern science, philosophy speaks to questions about the world in which we find ourselves. And, to the extent that theology also speaks to questions of this world, to that extent it cannot ignore what philosophy and the modern sciences have to say in regard to one's relation to others. That is so because religious questions are basically human questions; a relation to God is a human relation.

'The structure of belief in . . .'
For the first discourse to be different from the second, 'faith' cannot be in God. As already noted it has to be faith or belief in human others. In other words, we are looking for who I am, what my relation to you is like, when I believe or trust in you.

That which makes the first discourse different from the second is its subjects: 'we' and 'others'. Both are human. Believing in others is a process, an on-going thing with a structure, a body with members. What we want to pursue is the question: What is that 'structure' and which are its existential members? Again sentences one and parts of sentence three:

> When we recognize our incapacity to know others, we recognize simultaneously their existence, our own (to which we are returned) and a fundamental reciprocity between them and us . . . [A] poverty funds all communication. This poverty signifies in effect both the desire which unites us to others and the difference which separates us from them.

The constitution or structure drawing our attention is that of existence. We experience a fundamental being-in-the-world-with-others, being in relation to them. We can speak of that experience in terms of its structure and in terms of the members of that structure.

'Structure' brings to mind organizations with interactive parts, not static but moving or progressing – not only in space but also in time. Existentially, 'structure' connotes emergence or becoming, the kind of thing we mean when we speak of anything that actually or metaphorically grows – from crystals to plants, to pets, to bodies, to human relationships, to love.

The French words expressed by our words 'fundamental' and 'funds' tell us a bit more about the meaning of 'structure'. The images which come to mind are those of the foundation of a building or of a sum of money to support a project. In other words a firm basis, an architectural or monetary support. Or we may think of a 'constitution', as an assemblage of elements expressive of how a people organize their government or as how our physical bodies function. In other words, we imagine things organized or growing which may collapse or corrupt. According to the Pilgrim, 'structure' refers to a global social experience which is to flourish and grow.

'All communication ...'
What we refer to by 'all communication' is fundamental to existence. Given that importance, we take note of the phrase here and will return to it further on. Certeau chooses his words carefully. 'All communication' refers to any making known by means of a language or a system of signs used to give knowledge or to express feelings. Communication is 'verbal' and 'non-verbal' expressions which entail signs such as words and pictures. Communication may be taken to include receiving as well as sending; it is this subjective side which has most of our attention here. The Pilgrim tells us communication is part of a structure which is not only solidly funded for growth but also involves every kind of making known by means of language, verbal and non-verbal.

Where, in our existence, in our subjective experience of relation to others, do we begin to see the structure of belief in them?

'When we recognize our incapacity to know others ...'
Initially there's an experience, a going through something which evokes a recognition. A while ago I wrote that we experience a fundamental being-in-the-world-with-others. What does the Pilgrim have us note that clearly evokes the recognition that we are not alone? In the sentence which ends the paragraph immediately before the one we are studying, he answers: '[the] experience of resistance ...' Like a wall into which we walk, others may often differ with us.

Not itself one of the existential members of the structure of belief in others, their expressing resistance to the grasp of our ideas and wishes makes possible our discovery of those members. Whatever the reasons, a fact of our experience is the resistance or opposition of others to this or that idea or wish. In their relation to us, others resist not only by what they say or refuse to hear but also by what they do or refuse to see. How often we hear ourselves saying such things as, 'I don't get your drift' or, 'You are not doing what I said.' How often do we see a partner, a peer or a fellow professional go against what we – and we think society generally – expect to be done? Another driver does not observe an accepted rule of the road, no left turn, and we exclaim, 'You can't do that.' Yet resistance is not basically an issue of human bad will, it is an issue of who we are; we meet it not only with those hostile to us but with those who are ill, elderly, mentally challenged, any who are more limited in their existence than we.

You are riding with a friend. You are going somewhere neither of you has been before. Your friend, the driver, has a set of directions different from your own. The friend insists on following their directions and becomes lost. You say, 'Let's go back, and try my directions.' Your friend refuses, you remain lost. You say, 'This isn't working.' Still your friend insists their way has to be the way. You are powerless to change what is happening. You feel oddly confused and angry; you fall silent. After yet more useless driving around, your friend discovers the way you had originally proposed and asks, 'Why didn't you tell me?'

What I just described could happen to any of us. We have

a relation to an other, we have a goal shared by the other, but we also have two awkwardly opposed ideas about the way to get there. There is resistance (on both sides). In the example, the other in the driver's seat is in charge and is unable to listen. Reason will not change the driver; force is not an option. We may begin to feel like some inferior beside some kind of superior.

Resistance is that by which we recognize our inability to grasp others by what we hold and/or by what we wish. In the example, what we hold is an idea of our friend as someone who is like us in a particular way, who thinks as we do and who we want to do as we would if we were driving. But the friend is not like that. When others resist, it is not necessarily that they are hostile; their resistance may be friendly, like the Pilgrim to whom a companion once exclaimed, 'God is good!' and the Pilgrim surprised the companion, asking, 'How do you know that?'

Recognition

We recognize something fundamental in cases like the foregoing. If others often differ with us, they somehow always escape us. Recognition may take only one such experience or it may take many over time. Sooner or later we finally note something important, in particular about our ideas of others, ideas of what it is appropriate for them to say or do. Recognition or awareness may come in encounters of every kind. In *The Stranger* Certeau singles out encounters between those who are somehow in a minority and those who are somehow in charge, such as: missionaries with non-Christians, parents with children, teachers with students. All our lives, in those kinds of encounters, especially perhaps when we ourselves are part of some supposedly superior side, something particularly ordinary begs for our recognition.

'We recognize our incapacity to know others ...'
Here is the first member of the existential structure of belief in others. As a matter of fact, especially in the scientific

culture of today, what we know and understand about other human beings is always limited, incomplete, not total. As someone once remarked, 'All we know about anybody else is what we know about ourselves.' Certeau helps us to turn that around: all we know about ourselves is what we know about others. In the greater picture of reality this is very little. We are as poor in knowledge of ourselves as we are in knowledge of others.

It is not that we know nothing. At least, when it comes to facts, humans collectively know more today than anyone previously dreamed of knowing, black holes for example. And yet, even our collective knowledge does not add up to the knowable part of a whole, some of which may be wholly unknowable. It is that we lack the capacity to know all there is to be known. An idea that we do have such a capacity would postulate an unknown with known limits which is as a matter of fact knowledge we do not have. In a relation to others as well as to the cosmos, we have to recognize that we are always at the border between known and unknown, between a little and more. Day to day we may forget the border, even pretend it isn't there, but that does nothing to change the fact that it is there.

Forgetting or ignoring our fundamental ignorance seems to be one of the things driving arguments and even wars at the beginning of the twenty-first century. In debates about Darwinian evolution versus 'design' or about whether homosexuality is a matter of nature or nurture or about whether or not God exists, how often does either side begin by recognizing what they do not know about the other's side? How often do candidates for political office recognize what they do not know about others? Would it not make sense for such debates to begin with some recognition of that? Or are we so unhappy with our uncertainty that we must pretend it does not exist?

Our Guide once said to someone who told him of an other's wish to die, 'Psychological perversity is just beside the truth.' In other words, the dying person's true wish may have been to live. That suggests we ask whether the desire for certainty is a perversion of the desire to know. As Stephen Hawking has said, 'I've changed my mind. I'm now glad that our search for understanding will never come to an end.' That may be too true. In 'The Universe, Expanding Beyond All Understanding', an essay in the *New York Times* on 5 June 2007, Dennis Oberbye tells us:

> If things keep going the way they are, Lawrence Krauss of Case Western Reserve University and Robert J. Scherrer of Vanderbilt University calculate, in 100 billion years the only galaxies left visible in the sky will be the half-dozen or so bound together gravitationally into what is known as the Local Group; ... observers in our island universe will be fundamentally incapable of determining the true nature of the universe; ... it makes you wonder just how smug we should feel about our own knowledge. There may be fundamentally important things that determine the universe that we can't see, Dr. Krauss said in an interview. 'You can have right physics, but the evidence at hand could lead to the wrong conclusion. The same thing could be happening today.'

We can ask: Would it not be perverse to believe in a certainty built upon a denial of our incapacity or inability to fully grasp otherness, things as well as persons? Wouldn't that mean believing that what one is saying, that one's words are equivalent to or the same as what one is speaking of, that a word is the same as a thing? How could one affirm – contrary to experience – that what we say about or to one another is all there is to know, that there is nothing to wonder about, that there can be no surprises?

'Others ...'

We have finally to admit that others are strangers to us, just as we are to them. And we are strangers to ourselves. We can know ourselves no better than we know others. Evident in others' resistance to us, is our need to recognize our incapacity to know them, the first member in the structure of belief in others.

Much of what we know about ourselves today comes from the modern human sciences; thus, even from that point of view, what we know about ourselves is based upon an incomplete knowledge of others. The recent opening of the study of the human genome and the discoveries it may lead to is a dramatic evidence of the point. The recognition of our ignorance of others is therefore part of an answer to the question: Who am I?

How modern scientists illustrate the effect of recognizing our incapacity to know others is illustrated by Joseph Luft. In his *Introduction to Group Dynamics* (1955),[2] he schematizes what we know about others (and what they know about us) as follows.

There are things about others which both they themselves and we know. These things are shared. When something is known to an other and to oneself, it is said to be 'open to everyone'.

Some things about others to which they are blind, we are not. Those may include anything from peculiar habits to soup on someone's tie. When something is not known to an other but is known to oneself, we speak of the other's 'blind spot'.

Things about others to which we are blind, they may not be. Such things are 'partially known'. We never know everything knowable about an other – even when it is not a question of something they wish to keep a secret. When something knowable is known to an other but not to oneself, it is 'hidden from oneself'.

Many if not most things about humans (and the world, as well) are inaccessible both to others and to ourselves, and may always remain so. These things are unknown and perhaps unknowable to anyone of us. When something is known neither to an other nor to oneself, it is 'the unknown'. The unknown is immeasurable.

On both sides of every relationship there is a certain foundation for belief on the basis of uncertainty, on the basis of our recognition of our incapacity to know others, on the basis of the unknown which makes us all strangers.

Obstacles to belief in strangers

Language communication is most important in the Pilgrim's discourse on the structure of one's belief in others. Belief has to do with others' verbal and non-verbal expressions. Thus, along with our need to recognize our incapacity to know others, recognition of the role of language in how we take what they say and do is another, a second member of the structure of our belief in others.

Communication has to do with the 'reading' or reception of others' meaning. Thus obstacles to good reception are obstacles to belief in others. What is the key to good reception? Good listening. And yet, it is something we may not do automatically.

Listening well requires something humans have known a long time. The need is most obvious in relations which carry the hallmarks of mentor and learner. For example, in *The Stranger*, our Guide refers to parents-children, to teachers-students, and to missionaries with those to whom they are sent. ('Stranger' in French has also the meaning of the English word 'foreigner', used in the sense of outsiders to whom one goes for any reason.) Thus, a parent, a teacher or a missionary goes 'to the stranger' and is received (and resisted) as a stranger in a strange land.

In the sixteenth century, as the founder of the Jesuits who were missionaries as well as educators, Ignatius of Loyola may have gained insight into the need for listening as a stranger in a strange land when, after his mid-life religious conversion, visiting many lands, he began to converse with others about their beliefs. His insight into existential dialogue is so important to him that he makes it the presupposition of his *Spiritual Exercises* which he developed over many years. He says that one must be more ready to place a good rather than a bad interpretation upon the expressions of others.

It needs to be noted here that Ignatius was no fool about existence. He also adds that, when a good interpretation of an other's expressions is not possible, then their understanding should be questioned and kindly corrected. If that does not work, 'all appropriate means should be taken to bring them to a correct interpretation, and so defend a proposition from error'. He does not say which means are appropriate, but we can assume that today he would agree with the understanding that repressive and/or intimidating measures are in-appropriate, abusive of human dignity.

The questions we raise here are: How often, listening to an other, do I put more of a bad rather than a good interpretation on what they are saying? What would a readiness more to find others wrong than right tell us about ourselves?

A list of obstacles to listening well shows some of the ways we come to placing bad interpretations upon what others say. During the past century, thanks to clarifications from sciences like psychology and sociology, we are brought to recognize obstacles by the answers to questions like the following.

When an other is speaking to me: How much and how often is my mind on something I would rather be doing? How much of my attention is distracted by things like previous images I have of this person – am I thinking of things like: 'There she goes again'? How much do I expect him or her to express things my way, in words I would use rather than in their own words? How much of my energy goes not to hearing an other's meaning but rather to preparing a defence of my own idea, a rebuttal of the other's view? How much of my attention is diverted by a fear, for example, that I may have to say yes (or no) to a possible request?[3]

Whether it is a distracting agenda, a false image, a different language, a defensive posture or a worrisome anxiety, its effect will be the same. We will listen less attentively, we will be more likely to misconstrue the language of others. Experience may show that this is especially true in encounters between those who have known each other a long time. Familiarity may breed misunderstanding, for sure it fosters recognition of what we look at next.

'Their existence ...'

We continue our look at each word of the Pilgrim's philosophical discourse. By the resistance of others, we recognize the limits of our knowledge. With that we recognize that others exist. Just as we are, others are in the world with others. Recognition of others' existence is the third member of the structure of belief.

With the Pilgrim we recognize existence in a way different from but related to the ways of, for example, René Descartes or Albert Camus. Placed at the beginning of modern thought, in the seventeenth century René Descartes is reported to have inaugurated his view of existence, saying, 'I think therefore I am.' Distinguishing himself from Descartes, Albert Camus, a twentieth-century French existential philosopher, begins his own view or 'proof of' existence, not in the mind but outside it, not in the logic of a thinking subject but rather in the opposition of an active subject. Camus responded, 'I rebel, therefore I am.' Certeau continues the discussion by inaugurating his vision with an emphasis upon moments of resistance by others. His reply to Camus (and to Descartes) is, as I put it, 'You resist, therefore we are.' One immediately knows by the resistance of others that one is not alone.

'Simultaneously ...'
Those who study the habits of drivers of automobiles speak of 'reaction time'. Between my seeing an indicator light of a car beside mine and my reacting to the signal by slowing my car to allow the other car to move into place ahead of me, there is a measurable amount of time; this is true for all of us. There is nothing of the kind in the case of the recognition of which the Pilgrim writes. We know others exist at precisely the same moment as the one in which we recognize our inability to completely know them. There is no elapsed time between sensing a slap in the face and recognizing an other as other. Along with the recognition of our incapacity to know others and of their existence with us, there is simultaneous recognition of two other things.

'Our own (to which we are returned) ...'
Included in the third member is the recognition of one's own existence. As in the case of driving somewhere with a friend,

the existence of others often makes us notice our own. We are aware, at times painfully aware, of our being with an unreadable, perhaps hostile, stranger. Their resistance to us may irritate and/or fascinate, make us angry and/or unable to let go. Whichever it is, along with an admission of our incapacity to know them, their resistance evokes within us a heightened awareness of our existence, of being not alone, of being with others, and of grasping neither them nor ourselves. As in the case of the Pilgrim's resistant reply to his companion, recognition of our own existence means self-questioning: How indeed do I know that God is good?

A thousand years ago, thinking perhaps of Plato's description of Socrates, the Spanish Jewish philosopher Moses Maimonides made recognition of our incapacity the basis of becoming fully human. He said, 'Teach thy tongue to say "I do not know", and thou shalt progress.'

The experience of an other's questioning or downright refusal to conform to our way of thinking and doing can evoke self-questioning: What don't I know? What am I missing? What am I not doing right? What can I change? Uncertainty accumulates. At least for the moment, we may have to remain silent, because by the resistance of an other we are reminded of our incapacity to know them – and ourselves. We are reminded that they exist as we do. We may begin to learn other things about our existence. Recognizing that we do not know others opens us to learning. And, as the Pilgrim is about to show us, we discover another member of the structure of belief in others.

'A fundamental reciprocity ...'
An existentialist style focuses on existence, life as we experience it in relation to others. Existence, being in the world, belongs at the same time both to others and to oneself. I am not only in the world with a resistant other; an other is in the world with resistant me. Therewith is the fourth member of the structure we are exploring.

Existence is being in the world with others, but that is far from being passively next to them, like an egg in a carton.

Our Guide has a particular way of emphasizing the fact. He does this by adopting a particular phrase; existence, he writes, means not being in the world without others. The twentieth-century German philosopher Martin Heidegger is the Pilgrim's source for the phrase 'not without'.[4] We hear it said in one way or another every day. The words of lovers in poems and in popular songs come to mind: 'I miss you, I cannot live without you.' The Pilgrim reminds his readers of something Catholic faithful used to say in their service, at the time of communion: 'Never let me be separated from You.'

For the Pilgrim the phrase, 'not without', expresses his deepened existential insight. People in all sorts of relationships, not just lovers, say it, and all sorts of evidence to our senses shows it: very rarely if ever is anyone entirely alone, entirely without others. Life is all about being unable to do without resistant-existent others. We may be solitary or feel alone but even a hermit on Mount Athos is never wholly without others. From conception to death, to exist is being 'not without' others.

Another French existentialist, Jean-Paul Sartre, is famous for supposedly saying, 'Hell is others.' Certeau confesses others are strangers: resistant, unknown, even hostile. Although others may give us hell, I infer that to the Pilgrim hell they are not. If existence is good, others cannot be bad for, as Certeau writes in *The Stranger*, existence itself is received, a gift, whether we like it or not. Hell or Heaven is what one does with the gift.

The effect of reciprocity: communication as dialogue

Once, in a conversation about *The Stranger*, Certeau mentioned the Jewish existential philosopher Martin Buber.[5] The Pilgrim's sense of reciprocity parallels that of Buber.

Buber wrote of 'the life of dialogue'. Dialogue, a word from Greek, means literally two-words, two speakers. In dialogue there is a two-way give and take, and the experience is somehow the same for each side; we may suppose ideally that is when listening is nearly at its best. Buber also refers to dialogue as 'reciprocity'. It is communication in its deepest sense. It is existential, something our being with others cannot be without. It is a two-way give and take, somehow the same for both sides. For Buber it seems to refer to something even more radical than making known by means of language or a system of signs used to give knowledge or to express feelings.

For Buber, reciprocity involves us with others in a particular way. Buber writes that it is more than 'monologue', which to him is a way of living which 'even in the tenderest intimacy will not grope out over the outlines of the self'. In reciprocity, Buber says, an other 'is not my object, I have got to do with [the other]'. That is, the other is also a subject. In each relationship 'a word demanding an answer has happened to me'. As we have seen, the Pilgrim might speak of that differently: 'I see how a resistant other cannot do without me.'

For the Pilgrim, a life of belief in others means recognition of our poverty in the face of the resistance of others, but it also means something more: a kind of lack, a being without, which is shared, reciprocal, a part of others' existence as well as of one's own. Recognition of this reciprocity is the fourth subjective member of the structure of our belief in others.

'Fundamental ... between them and us ...'

In our reading of the philosophical language of our Guide's text, we find reciprocity underlies our existence, our being-with-others. It is not only one more of the members which structure or constitute our experience of belief in others, it is also basic to it. It is fundamental, foundational; to the extent it is absent, the structure of belief is weakened. Without reciprocity it would be as if no one is there. As with listening, to the extent that reciprocity is not there, communication is limited, exchange of meaning is corrupted. To the extent that communication fails, belief in the other is crippled. Thus, reciprocity is as basic to belief or trust as it is to communication.

Language communication is two-way, a give and take between oneself and an other, between equals. We are equals to the extent that we recognize the limits of our knowledge, our lack of what an other may know. Our equality means that any 'top-down' attitude toward others, implying that I-know-all-and-you-do-not, denies one's fundamental reciprocity (because it denies one's poverty).

Reciprocity and communication in Buber's description seem linked as two sides of one coin are linked. On the one hand, underlying reciprocity involves silence. We can see that by using an image which Buber gives to illustrate the reciprocity of dialogue. He writes, 'I ... think of something unpretentious yet significant – of the glances which strangers exchange in a busy street as they pass one another with unchanging pace.' On the other hand, he says, 'an element of communication no matter how inward seems to belong to its essence'. Existence is actual life, and 'all actual life is encounter'. Existence involves the sounds of speech.

Recognizing our incapacity to know others means recognizing that we are alike: united by what we do not know. Both communication and reciprocity refer to exchange, give and take. Something about the constitution of existence is the same for both sides in any encounter or exchange. Neither side is the object of the other; each is a subject addressed in a relationship of an I to a You, each existentially equal to the other.

As we are about to see, we share the radical equality of difference. First, we have to see that we share something else. Elsewhere in *The Stranger,* Certeau writes, 'to exist is ... to encounter before one-self, like an unreadable or hostile face, the presence of other liberties ...'[6] Communication between equal subjects means reciprocal recognition not only of reciprocity itself but also of some essential modes of the subjective existence of others and therefore of oneself. One of these modes is liberty, which may be described as a subject's ability to choose or not to choose to take or not to take this or that step which one judges to be right or wrong in relation to things as well as to others (the environment as well as neighbours). More to the point in the present context would be a particular sense of freedom given it by Camus when he says, 'Freedom is the ability to admit that your opponent may be right'. (See: Olivier Todd, Albert Camus, A Life, 1997.) To exist is to be in the world with others, equal liberties like

Who Am I? 39

oneself. But equality in liberty is not the only basic of subjective existence noted by Certeau. Two more are noted in the portion of his discourse we are about to examine.

Communication which is genuine

Recognizing our 'poverty', a lack or want in our knowledge of others, means recognizing existential reciprocity between free and equal subjects. Reciprocity is expressed in language. To the extent that language is all there is between us, its essence or soul is reciprocity. The poverty underlying it is the first thing we have to keep in mind when we come to sentence three of Certeau's philosophical discourse. In it the Pilgrim tells us that our existential human incapacity speaks and that, 'This poverty signifies in effect both the desire which unites us to and the difference which separates us from others ...'

'This poverty ...'
Before a word is spoken, recognizing our 'want' or 'lack' of knowing others helps decide whether reciprocal communication will be genuine. To what extent can communication be genuine rather than pretending?

To the extent that communication is based upon any denial of our incapacity to know others it is perverse, just beside the truth. In *The Stranger*, the Pilgrim suggests examples. Pretence is the kind of thing we sometimes sense in conversations touching on political and/or religious issues. Others expect to hear from us whatever they believe they know. Their pretence is that we are the same as they. On the other hand we may hear ourselves echoing (in our own words) what we believe others expect to hear from us. Our pretence is that we are the same as they.

Our attitudes may involve a psychological factor of group or peer 'pressure'. Along with our Guide, what we want to note is what may go along with such pressure. There may be an attempt to conquer and/or to pacify. On the one hand, it is a patronizing insistence that others see things our way by telling them their words mean the same as ours. On the other hand, in conversations touching upon socially important issues, pretending to listen is a way of having a good conscience. We let an other speak, say all they wish. But we are focused upon any and every obstacle to really hearing them. And, when they have finished, we go on with our own monologue as if nothing had happened.[7]

Psychologists might tell us more about the meaning of such pretence. From the point of view of the Pilgrim, it would seem to go against something very human signified by authentic belief in others.

'Signifies in effect ...'

Our poverty by its effects speaks of ourselves. What is announced is seen in the eyes of a good man at the end of the German film *The Lives of Others*. Through a very particular expression, a look in the eyes, his poverty, like that of each of us, speaks of two essential modalities behind all communication. Such expressions are not reducible to either their signifier (poverty) or to the modalities (desire and difference) of which they are the effects. To those two modalities of who we are we now turn.

'Both the desire which unites us to others ...'

There is a desire for others even if we spend much of our day alone. Whether it is called need or want, it is there. It goes with the existential fact that we do not exist without them. It is so much a part of us that, try as we might to untie ourselves, we remain bound to others. Before we are inclined to see any need or want which an other might fill, this desire signifies a good curiosity which is not minding others' business, but rather desiring to know them. The sense of human desire is both scientific and biblical, both a desire for understanding and a desire for union. Could one even say that it is a desire to know what they know as they themselves may know it? As noted earlier, Certeau said shortly before his death that this desire eternally oscillates between the desire to possess and to be changed by an other. Psychological factors may pervert this desire contributing to pretence and an effort to fulfil the desire in wrong ways; but is it ever really gone from anyone?

'And the difference which separates us from them ...'
Beside an obviously selfish (perhaps self-protective) concern for our own, different ideas and wishes there is a way in which everyone is unselfishly outstanding. It is so obvious it is hidden in plain sight. It is quite simple; it shows what our fingerprints show, that no one is the same as anyone else. At the end of *The Lives of Others*, a former member of the East German secret police has left identification with that police role and found his way to a simple but more authentic existence with others, a strengthening of his difference.

Each of us is a difference. Our difference is what separates or distinguishes us. It is how we are with others. Where a more essentialist philosopher may speak of a 'principle of individuation', our Guide speaks of what I call an existential principle of differentiation. 'Individual' and 'difference' in this context are synonyms. Difference is that which funds all our particular individuality. Along with liberty and desire it is an essential modality of who we are, of our being with others. So, what is mine is not yours and never can be. It is my birth and my body-mind, my life and my death.

We not only want to be with others, we want to be who we are with them: different, ourselves. That is the other thing our poor incapacity to know signifies by anything we say or do. And, if our lack of knowledge unites us, our difference gives us distance. Distance means separation, a gap which we are ever trying to close, which we never do.

Perhaps even without our recognizing it, our poverty signifies in effect not only an essential want, a desire to 'be with' others, but also an equally essential individuality, a being different from them. Together with equality in liberty, uniting desire and separating difference have prominent membership in the structure of belief. From the point of view of liberties in relation to other liberties, our desire is inseparable from our difference. Both are signified in the communication of belief and love, in word and in deed.

'All communication ...'
Communication is genuine when there is no pretence, when what is signified is reverence, holding in deep, even affectionate respect, not only the uniting desire but also the separating difference of another subject. To the extent that we grow in that respect, the more genuine our communication becomes, because to that extent we have to recognize what we do not know; our uncertainty about this or that.

We have come to a point where we may say that expressed belief in what other liberties hold both unites us to and separates us from them. This is so since communication, language (verbal and non-verbal expression), is ultimately all there is between us. It is also so when perchance we somehow say, 'I don't believe what you are saying', a saying which by itself does not necessarily deny a desire for union but does necessarily affirm difference.

Any language we use always falls short of being adequate to what it attempts to speak of. This is due to the fact of our fundamental poverty and the fact that no sign is ever the same as the thing it refers to. Is there more to our poverty than our incapacity to know others and the limits of signs we use to communicate our desire?

We return to some words at the end of sentence two. When recognized, poverty permits us to recognize existence as well as its fundamental reciprocity. Most of all it funds questions. Therefore, poverty affects communication. Thus far, we have treated the word poverty as though it refers only to a want of knowledge of others. Certeau writes, '[A] poverty ... underlies all communication.'

Does poverty include more than a want of knowledge of others? What does the word 'all' tell us? Communication is not only about knowledge of others; it is also about knowledge of the otherness of the world in which we live. As experience and modern science teach us, we are poor, we want knowledge, not just of others but also of the world we inhabit with them. We are tied to and separated from others also in regard to want of that knowledge. It is by them that we learn about the world. And so, the existential poverty of knowledge underlying all our communication includes what others disclose not only about their or our selves but also about the universe and everything. All communication falls within our believing or trusting in others.

Furthermore, as we shall see, our existential poverty of knowledge, our not-knowing, also speaks silently of some other, immeasurable, more profound want of knowing; that is, of our lack of knowledge of the Other referred to as God. And there our lack is truly immeasurable.

Who am I?

Since the structure of belief in others is grounded in a poverty, the way of speaking which represents it best is speaking questions. Thus we see why the Pilgrim was known as someone who 'stood in the question'. Also, we know that, to the extent that each human maintains that humble pattern in their relation with others, they too become those who stand in the question.

Long ago, Socrates stood for being aware of what one does not know. Consistent with that, the first member of the structure of belief in others is recognizing our incapacity for knowledge of others even by their words or deeds, verbal or non-verbal language. What one knows of others can be taken for what one knows of oneself. What you or I know of ourselves is, relatively little. A recent report says scientists are on the verge of decoding Neanderthal DNA to show how it differs from ours. The report says, 'Those differences ... essentially spell out in biological terms what makes humans human.' My point is that there will always be more to be known in answer to what makes us human. Not only in biological but in psychological, sociological, and in so many other terms.

On the other hand, we can note that our sketch of the structure of belief in others indicates the constitution of a subjective attitude or habit: a trust in others which is modest, attentive and caring. Belief begins and ends with not knowing others. Not knowing may be described metaphorically as a kind of darkness or blindness; it is enlightened or made better when coupled with a respectful, maybe educated, willingness to question anything that is said or done. Such an attitude is exemplified by the Pilgrim. It is a generous curiosity. Due to human desire for union, curiosity is best when also joined by a modest but ordinary willingness to be more ready to put a positive rather than a negative construction upon the words and deeds of others. At the same time questioning is obviously incompatible with a willingness to believe anything.

A global, existential, fundamental structure

What we have been glossing or commenting upon is these words in our Guide's first discourse:

> When we recognize our incapacity to know others, we recognize simultaneously their existence, our own (to which we are returned) and a fundamental reciprocity between them and us ... [A] poverty ... funds all communication. This poverty signifies in effect both the desire which unites us to others and the difference which separates us from them ...

In some detail we have tried to understand parts of a structure and how they fit together. We have noted five inter-related members of our subjective experience, all having to do with who any one of us is.

We have noted:

1. a limit of our knowing,
2. the central role of language communication,
3. the existence of others as well as of ourselves, and
4. a mutual interdependence between them and ourselves.
    We have also recognized that others are
5. fundamentally equal to us in liberty, desire and difference.

Thus we have disclosed a little more fully the global, existential, and fundamental structure of belief in others as the Pilgrim speaks of it in the first discourse of his paragraph in *The Stranger*. What we have developed is a sketch of the structure of belief in others. It is global, because it is true for humans anywhere. It is existential because it characterizes a human relation to others – to exist means recognizing our incapacity to know others which is fundamental to belief in them. To the extent that poverty is recognized, a questioning belief enters all human intercourse with others.

We have tried to see the structure of belief in terms of our experience as subjects in communication with other human subjects. Along with others, I am one who believes in them to the extent that I recognize my incapacity to know them. The phrase, 'to the extent', alerts us to a key element in sentence two of our Guide's philosophical discourse. It goes with a sixth member of the structure of belief in others. To that we next turn. It deals with action from a position defined by the existential structure we have been examining.

Questions

Am I convinced that understanding human existence as 'being-in-the-world-with others' is a fertile starting point for building an anthropology, an understanding of human life?

The structure of belief in others has so far been referred to, somewhat artificially, in terms of 'five members'. The reference is nly for the sake of easier understanding. In my own words, how would I describe or explain the five members of the existential structure of belief in others? In addition to them, why do I think equality in liberty is important? Even though the Pilgrim does not include liberty in his paragraph, do I think it should be considered a member of the structure of belief in others? Why?

What happens when we believe? What happens the moment a companion confesses to an other 'I believe in you' or a People tells others, 'We believe you are our equal in liberty'? Our reading of Certeau allows us to think that, in the moment of saying those things, we recognize particular facts of life. What are they? Do they coincide with what you find in your own experience of belief in others?

Can any one of the members of the structure be without any one of the others? Why must those members belong together? Familiarity can breed disbelief in the sense that others whom we think we 'know' can surprise and disappoint us, sometimes painfully. Should such disappointment be fatal to or bring to an end one's belief in an other? Why or why not?

Notes

1. Macquarrie, John, *Existentialism*, New York, Pelican, 1973. See also his *Thinking About God*, New York, Harper and Row, 1975. These books are useful for appreciating some important aspects of the thinking of contemporaries of which Certeau was certainly aware.
2. Luft, Joseph, *Group Processes, An Introduction to Group Dynamics*, Palo Alto, National Press, 1970.
3. Howe, Reuel L., *The Miracle of Dialogue*, New York, Seabury, 1963.
4. Certeau, 'How is Christianity Thinkable Today?'
5. Buber, Martin, *Between Man and Man*, New York, Macmillan, 1966.
6. *L'étranger*, p. 20. The passage: *'Exister, c'est recevoir d'autri l'existence, mais c'est aussi, en sortant de l'indifférentiation, provoquer ses réactions; c'est être accepté et adhérer à société, mais aussi prendre position à son égard et rencontrer devant soi, comme un visage illisible ou hostile la présence d'autres libertés.'*
7. *L'étranger*, p. 166.

Chapter 3

Union in Difference

The salt rebuff of speech,
Insisting so on difference, made me welcome:
Once that was recognized, we
were in touch.

Philip Larkin

We are following the Pilgrim, looking at reality through the window of philosophy. We are exploring the existential structure of belief in others; that is, the subjective foundation for a habit or attitude of belief in them. We are noticing things common to all of us in relation to others. We are focused primarily on the subjective side of inter-subjective existence with its inter-play and inter-change of uniting desire and separating difference. We are looking at the 'members' of the structure of subjective belief in others, at some of its connection to language, to what is between us.

We began by noting that existence often means meeting the resistance of others. We know their resistance – and they know ours – through verbal and non-verbal languages. Neither they nor we always say and do the expected thing, we differ – sometimes violently. In *The Stranger,* our Guide writes of conflict as a 'law of existence', something we can do nothing about. But we can do something about how we respond under the law. We can try to adhere more to the structure of belief in others. We can try to live more by the wisdom of uncertainty; that is, by standing in the question which emerges from our poverty: What don't I know?

The Pilgrim shows us a fundamental choice: by the resistance of others, do I recognize an obstacle to be beaten away or, along with my incapacity to grasp them (and myself), do I recognize an unknown? Is hostile as well as ordinary resistance something to be overcome or the occasion for progress? That is, how well do I recognize the foundation of the structure of belief in others, of a way of uncertainty? Its horizon is the known at which we may too often and too easily take as the end, when just over the horizon there is the unknown.

With belief in others, humans bring a particular way of looking at them. What that way is we see in sentence two of the Pilgrim's paragraph. Before we resume our detailed consideration of the Pilgrim's words about the structure of belief in others, we look a bit more at how he lets us understand difference.

Difference and differences

Harmony is only part of the picture of the relationship of belief in others. In one's relation to an other, the downside of difference is that it inevitably leads to differences or conflicts. A 'law of conflict' means resistance, differences, the source of which is difference.

Modern science has taught us useful things to add to our understanding difference. The human sciences give us many objective findings about it. Through the windows of sociology, psychology and biology, we see how complex and rich separating difference is when it comes to our desired union with others. We learn about mind, body, languages – our habits, words and deeds.

What we learn about difference through scientific windows is given a suggestive summary by Dr D. H. Donnelly under the heading of 'human difference'.[1] We can look at human Culture, Education, Environment, Experience and Expectations, CE4 or 'See-level' for short. Those encompass many findings which we know shape our views, how we see and do things. 'See-level' or

CE4 refers to the nutrients not determinants of differentiation. See-level means Culture or one's habits, Education or one's learning, Environment or one's body, Experience or one's story, and Expectations or one's hopes and dreams. See-level enters into the story of every life, of every difference becoming actually, more completely, existentially what they are – different from all others. Thinking of past or present human difference according to the scientific objective sense of any those basics fits well with the existential subjective sense of our Guide.

Philosophical or 'existential difference' does not refer to the things summarized under 'human difference'. 'Existential difference' refers to any one of us simply as individuals in relation to others, whereas See-level refers to what is known about us through scientific study using objects such as 'unconscious mechanisms', 'peer group pressure', our 'genome', and so on. At the same time, the results of scientific study can and must contribute to better understanding of one's self and of one's many-sided relation to others, especially in conflict. We have already noted how scientific study of behaviour sheds light on obstacles to listening to others. Conflicts are effects with deep roots in our existence, in what we are: desire and difference. We have to learn effectively that obstacles make up some part of our own resistance. To learn to listen well is to learn to lessen the effect of that resistance, but not to end differences.

Turning to another aspect of understanding difference, we note that competing needs for union and difference can be difficult to balance. Of the two, Certeau draws our attention to something we all recognize in ordinary experience. In a passage of *The Stranger* referred to above, he writes of 'leaving un-differentiation'. He says, 'To exist is to receive existence from an other, but it is also, in leaving un-differentiation, to provoke reactions; it is to be accepted in and to adhere to a society, but also to take a position in regard to it . . .' (See note 6 of the previous chapter for the French version of this sentence.)

'Un-differentiation' refers to anything without distinctions. An egg in a carton is 'undifferentiated' from its neighbour.

Any solid colour like solid red or blue or yellow is undifferentiated. An habitually pessimistic person, seeing only the dark side of things, has an undifferentiated outlook on life. While 'leaving un-differentiation' does not mean an egg becomes something other than an egg, it does mean getting out of the carton and becoming hard-boiled, not imitating one becoming scrambled. (The ancient idea of the imitation of Christ means, as St Paul writes, putting on the mind of Jesus, thinking in the differentiated way he thought, rather than trying to become a saviour.) Leaving un-differentiation is an aspect of living, growing difference; it is what difference does. It is what we have found ourselves doing when we have taken positions opposed to those of some group, such as family, social organizations or society generally. It is the formation of difference and also, together with the structure of belief, it is making room for other differences. It is what happens when who one is, difference, is nurtured: one grows, learns and paradoxically becomes more what one is, differentiated from as well as united with other differences.

As experience tells us, someone always resists some piece of how any union operates. This is true in conversations, in families, in classrooms and in societies, great and small. Parents know leaving un-differentiation from expressions of their teenage offspring, maturing differences. In the 1960s, as a teacher of government with a class of seventeen-year-olds, I had one student who sincerely espoused neo-Nazism. That year there was plenty of leaving un-differentiation (for both of us). Once I landed in one of the world's airports. On the long walk to baggage claim, a young man lit a cigarette. Perhaps because I am an ex-smoker, I asked him about his behaviour, violating the many 'No Smoking' signs. He said he had not agreed to that rule. Evidently he weighted difference preferable to union under the law. Leaving un-differentiation can go to extremes, emphasizing difference at the expense of union. On the other hand, where would any society be without those within it who in effect struggle – perhaps artlessly – for more respect for difference?

Thus, leaving un-differentiation is growing difference,

shedding sameness – hopefully for better and not for worse. Members of any union, from family to classroom to office to nation, experience its real effects. Even when we, you and I, are accepted in and adhere to this or that union, sooner or later we may find that in order to be ourselves we have to take particular positions. Alone or with others we take sides, assume points of view in regard to various issues. Thus we may come to disagree. Given our poverty, and the progressive way we learn, this is not surprising.

Given its ordinariness in any union, what is surprising is the extent to which humans will go to control, even to eliminate, difference. To the extent that the effects of leaving un-differentiation are genuine effects, expressing a desire to know based upon the recognition of our poverty, they are necessary to any union. Nevertheless, experience teaches us that, in the face of differences, others find ways to resist, to limit or to end them. Such ways are dangerous when and to the extent that resisting difference means repressing and/or eradicating, others' leaving un-differentiation. Humans have learned quite well the ways of pursuing that goal.

With the Pilgrim we look to existence as well as to modern science for ideas about how to understand difference within the structure of belief in others. What else do we look for? Existence, being with others, is dynamic; change is always a factor. Basic to our being is the need to become who one is. With the Pilgrim we are describing the growth of difference as 'leaving un-differentiation'. Leaving un-differentiation is both subjective and inter-subjective; we grow up and we grow away. In sentence two of the Pilgrim's philosophical discourse, he makes us think fundamentally about caring for differentiation in union with others.

Sentence two

Does any practical consequence go with recognition of the five members of the structure of belief? To conclude the description of its members at those five would leave the structure theoretical, without practice. Without ways and means, no goal is attainable. Our Guide describes a sixth member of the structure of belief. What he describes indicates practical means to the goal of the structure. When we do as indicated, we keep in sight not only difference, with its need to leave undifferentiation, but also the complement to difference, desire, with its need not to be without others. In sentence two, the Pilgrim writes,

> To the extent we agree *not to identify with anything others can expect of us and not to identify them with any satisfactions and assurances we hope to draw from them* we discover the sense of the *poverty* which funds all communication ...
> (Certeau's italics)

We resume our detailed consideration of the Pilgrim's words about the structure of belief in others with an easily missed but instructive aspect of everyday experience. The Pilgrim reminds us of a certain proportion in existence.

'To the extent ...'

The second sentence begins by drawing attention to a kind of proportion in our experience of existence, in our relation to others. The Pilgrim expresses the proportion in a negative way. Simply put, he says that the less we do one thing, the more we do another. The absence of one thing may signify the presence of another.

What the negative construction seems to emphasize is the prevalence of a tendency which certainly exists in experience. We may see others (and ourselves) as objects to be 'handled' or 'treated' rather than as others, as different subjects. A doctor expresses seeing others as objects in this way:

> Recently, I cared for a man in the emergency room. He was middle aged and alcoholic. A sour stench confirmed his claim that he lived in the woods ... Disgusted, I ... admitted him and ordered an alcohol detox protocol, but offered him little else ... I had made ... certain he got the indicated treatment; but I had missed *him*.[2] (Author's italics)

The doctor 'treated' the man properly; but from the Pilgrim's point of view, he had shown little belief in the man (as, perhaps, the man had shown little in the doctor). Besides reminding us of how we at times behave, the illustration also shows us that the context for what we are thinking is not necessarily a moralistic one, not about bad versus good persons. Neither the man nor the doctor are bad persons. While the behaviour of each lacks something important, the behaviour of neither the doctor nor the man comes anywhere near the criminal. Unfortunately, that is not always the case.

'We agree ...'
This clause brings us to our human social and political See-level, to the things society adds to existence, and in particular to agreements or practical arrangements made by persons in every kind of society, from couples to whole nations. Our focus is on ways the balance between the necessary and legitimate aims of union and difference is lost.

It was once popular to say, 'Half of us is u'. A relationship is a union of two relations, each one with many sides or aspects. A society is a union of many relationships, of many different subjects to many others. A source of resistance in our society is the presence of two competing aims on each side of a relationship. The aim of desire is union; the aim of difference is separation. These aims affect what is actually done, even perhaps in spite of agreed practical arrangements.

In *The Stranger* Certeau indicates two extreme ways in which societies may unbalance the aims of union and difference, largely at the expense of difference. He writes, 'Where there is no union, difference is inert; it is no longer the ferment of sense. But union becomes sterile and insignificant if it does not continually quicken the difference which brings it into question.'[3] 'Sense' may be taken both as theoretical understanding or meaning and as practical goal or purpose.

Outside a union, alone, a difference is 'inert'; one has little or no effect upon others. Within a union, to the extent that a difference is frowned upon or disappeared, difference is 'sterile and insignificant', one can neither produce nor express anything for others to peruse or to pursue. Absent from a society, difference has no effect upon that society. Repressed within a society (by ambition or intimidation), difference again has no effect. The removal of a whole group of differences, the Jews, from Hitler's Germany exemplifies removing difference from a society by making arrangements for something else, the worst effects of Nazi anti-Semitism. The silent inactivity of those Germans who thought 'the final solution' wrong was due to the presence of those with the power to induce fear.

In the second sentence of the paragraph under examination, the Pilgrim says in effect that, to the extent that differences are either ended within or excluded from a union, it literally loses life. In regard to the way to that loss, he speaks of two principle, subjective habits, manners of viewing self or others, which contribute to difference's being silenced within and/or disappeared from a society. We look at them one at a time.

'To identify ourselves with anything others can expect of us . . .'
While the Pilgrim writes of this as something to be done as little as possible, in reality it may seem an attractive choice. Life promises to be so much easier when I go along to get along, when I agree to express what's expected. In the extreme, identification means giving to those who are able to demand it, one's complete conformity in word and deed, no questions asked. To the extent that such agreement is given, it eliminates and/or excludes legitimate expressions of difference. To that extent agreement to conformity is untrue to the structure of belief in others.

Conforming may seem the best way to go, especially to the powerless. With not a little reason Benjamin Franklin said, 'Democracy is two wolves and a lamb deciding what to have for lunch.' A powerful majority can work like that. To the extent that it is wolves who decide the menu, lambs may think it better to run with the pack, perversely differentiating themselves by wearing wolves' clothing. Collaboration in this way is conformity at its worst.

Subjectively, conformity may seem quite right as well as safe. Often it truly is. Without agreed rules of the road, how much more dangerous would driving be? But in driving, the social agreement and aim is cooperation among differences. (Unfortunately, in driving, this is sometimes lost sight of.) Surrendering difference is not a positive form of cooperation. As we see in the German film, *The Lives of Others*, during the period of communist control in East Germany, people were oppressed by what was expected of them. Their oppression was enforced by watchers, the Stasi or secret police. With power aiming to exclude particular expressions of difference, it was safer to go along, even if one (silently) believed that what was happening was wrong. Conformity, identifying oneself with what others expect, is not necessarily to be a lamb acting as a wolf; nor is it done necessarily at the expense of denying one's difference. Yet, when identifying is acting the wolf or pretending undifferentiated sameness, the effect upon a society is the same; some of its life dies.

'To identify others with any satisfactions or assurances we hope to draw from them ...'
Again our Guide is writing of something we ought to agree not to do. Again what is described may be more characteristic of the powerful in a society (but not only of them). It is expecting conformity not of oneself but rather of others. Identifying others with what might be taken from them is seeing them foremost as suppliers of wants. Identifying in this way is seeing others less in terms of the subjects they are and more in terms of objects they can supply. It is in effect valuing others more for what can be got from them than for what they are in themselves: other differences. Others may be strangers not only in the sense of the alien (the outsider) but also in the sense of the neighbour (the insider). Identifying strangers with objects is valuing them less as equal liberties and more as means to the accumulation of whatever is deemed to satisfy and assure.

What satisfactions and assurances do we normally hope to draw from others? We find satisfaction and assurance in seeing and hearing what we have agreed to expect from each other. Materially that may mean goods and what comes with them: wealth and pleasures. Spiritually it may mean position and what comes with it: honours and influence. To the extent that such agreements comprise legitimate, mutual expectations, they are benign in regard to difference. We recall such agreements on the street. For example, they guide our driving habits. We remind one another at home; agreements guide how we live together as families. We learn them at work; they control who does which tasks. We find them in international relations; they should guide how nations behave towards one another. Mutual agreements are a glue of any union. Some expected satisfactions and assurances are ordinary and normal.

On the other hand, when ones hears suggestions to the effect that one is disloyal or obstructive because one does not go along with this or that authoritative expectation, or when what is to be said and done in this or that group or union is limited to this or that 'correct' or authoritative expression, then one rightly suspects an assault on difference. Strangers of every stripe are vulnerable to this.

The threat is worse when expectations somehow express an aim to limit, to silence or to repress difference so that there can only be what is already agreed, expected or allowed, known or believed. The alcoholic served by the doctor was seen by the doctor in this way. True, the alcoholic's behaviour was unacceptable, beyond what is agreed to be normal; however the doctor's disapproval tended to reject not only the alcoholic's behaviour but the man himself, his unknown difference. That is how even legitimate expectations of others go wrong.

Equally assaultive upon belief in others is when one is expected to believe that some question is completely answered and that to question the answer is automatically out of bounds. By giving into such a dogmatic or intolerantly authoritative position, one agrees that an other or some others have what no one else is able to have. Such concession goes against the foundation of belief in others; it is conforming to a demand to accept that a particular other has unquestionable knowledge of

Union in Difference   57

the unknown. It is a surrender to the abuse of difference. And with it of language, for what is allowed is only the repetition of what supposedly everyone has already agreed to say and/or to do, in spite of the unknown surrounding what is expected.

In other words, to the extent that we do identify ourselves and others more as objects than as subjects, what do we discover? First and most obviously, we discover nothing about the sense of our poverty and existence, since that discovery comes with seeing others more as subjects. We discover that our poverty has no sense. We discover the nonsense or existential 'absurdity' or pointlessness of which some existentialists speak.

'Not to identify ...'
The behaviour described in sentence two points to a positive discovery, the result of a positive step. What we discover by that step is the sense of our poverty and therefore the sense of belief in others, the sense of all communication. What are the step and the discovery?

Sentence two refers to a kind of conversion, a radical shift in one's difference and so also in one's See-level. The shift is necessary for the integrity and actuality of the structure of belief; to the extent that the shift is incomplete, the structure is weakened. The structure of belief requires the conversion. Given difference, neither I nor you can be reduced to this or to that thing, to one or another object. Our vision of ourselves and others may have often to move from focusing upon objects to focusing upon another subject.

The more one's vision is converted, the more scales fall from one's eyes, the more the goal of belief comes into clearer focus. A discovery is enhanced by action. As the Pilgrim once said, 'The important thing is to do something.' Can difference, division, resistance really have constructive meaning or direction, good sense? That is, to the extent that we do not identify ourselves and others with expected satisfactions and assurances, what is it we are doing? What is permitted? What is its sense? What brings union into question and quickens or enlivens it? What do they do who not only adhere to but also, by leaving un-differentiation, take a position within a group?

Following the Pilgrim of language, our focus is on communication or dialogue. With it we are most human, in verbal and non-verbal exchanges of meaning. Then, not to identify with expectations is fundamentally to reject any idea that we know more than we actually do, especially about ourselves and others. In one's relation to others, not to identify is like awareness in listening or in caring.

Listening well is receptiveness at its best, it is when one is aware of an other's expressions as theirs, existentially different from one's own. It is seeking and hearing in an other's words the other's meaning rather than that of some group. It is seeking in their behaviour their wants rather than those of their group. It is as far as possible seeing what they say and do differently not only as matters of fact but also as matters of value, as things worth wanting. Listening well is always done with open ears, open mind and closed mouth.

Caring is a particular kind of giving. As analysed by Milton Meyerhoff,[4] caring is helping an other to grow, to develop as the fundamentally different other they are. It is respect for the other's existence as the other's own. It is helping an other to leave un-differentiation, even at the risk of having to face questions to which one has no answer, questions which threaten one's senses of satisfaction and security.

Listening and caring are effects of viewing others' existence as their own and, as far as possible, viewing their existence neither wholly nor even partially as one's own or for one's use. Like listening and caring, not identifying is, in a phrase of the Pilgrim, 'making room for the other', for difference. It is in effect the opposite of bias and prejudice. Bias and prejudice are effects of favourable or unfavourable feelings toward others based on hearsay, jumping to conclusions, unexamined assumptions, and the law of the group. In regard to ourselves and others, not to identify by means of expectations of satisfactions and assurances is going against bias and prejudice by looking more toward the unknown, toward further differentiation, rather than toward the authoritatively known, the same, the familial, the domestic (in its national sense).

In regard to international relations, *New York Times* columnist David Brooks comes closer than he knows to agreeing with the Pilgrim when, concerning the confrontation between the West and the Muslim world, he writes: 'What we have is not a clash of civilizations, but a gap between civilizations, increasingly without common narratives, common goals or means of communication.'[5] What the gap signifies is the unknown, unrecognized by either side. (We will say more about such a gap in the final chapter.)

In other words, to the extent that we do not identify ourselves and others with any satisfaction or assurance which can be expected, we are not only recognizing our incapacity to know others and our reciprocity, but also we are in effect showing, as far as circumstances allow, unconditional acceptance of and respect for their difference. Showing such acceptance and respect is synonymous with doing what is called love. Therefore, to the extent that we do not identify ourselves and others as objects, we love. For Christians, this means that, to the extent possible, into every familial, friendly, professional and political calculation must enter consideration of Jesus' insistence that in order to love, one must do good to the different, the resistant liberty, the enemy.

Are we doing anything else? According to the Pilgrim, love is a modality of belief. Thus, to love others is to believe in them. Consequently, love of or belief in others is actually discovering the sense of the poverty funding all communication, finding sense in differences or conflicts. But we still have not answered: What is that sense?

The sense of differences in union

Does our endlessly finding only limited answers and always new questions have any sense, meaning or direction; and, if it does, what is it? The Pilgrim tells us there is a sense to be discovered. In mutual exchanges, to the extent that we adhere to our confession of the poverty of our knowledge, to the extent that we are accepted in and adhere to unions (from private to local to global), we leave un-differentiation in those unions, and to the extent that we identify neither ourselves nor others with the expectations of this or that particular union, then:

'We discover the sense of the poverty which funds all communication ...'
It is the sense of who we are together when all the existential members which structure belief in others are free to inter-act. The meaning or goal is not one's own difference; even though life is for learning and we can always differentiate ourselves. As a goal that would assert one's own difference alone. Nor is the meaning or goal exclusively this or that particular union; such limiting of the goal denies the global reach of our poverty. Rainer Maria Rilke wrote: 'Love consists in this, that two solitudes protect and border and salute each other.'[6] For 'solitudes' we can substitute 'differences'. Like love, belief tries to be unconditional. Belief in others is neither about fixing once and for all answers to questions, not about ending differences forever. Fixing or ending are paths to eliminating or repressing difference for the sake of exclusive and/or inclusive satisfactions and assurances. Belief in others is not about union or difference. It is not about union and difference. As long as differences flourish in unions, union in difference flourishes. That is the sense, direction or meaning, which we discover to the extent that we do not identify ourselves and others with expected satisfactions and assurances, do not close ourselves to the unknown. Belief or trust begins and ends with the unknown. To the extent our communication signifies our desire to know the unknown and the differentiation or distinguishing of ourselves, it is the way to the sense of existence. The existential sense, the persistent goal of the way of uncertainty or of standing in the question, and so of the structure of belief in others, is union in difference.

Given the goal of human belief in others, we turn in the next chapter to how the Pilgrim lets us see one particular believer in others and what we may gather from the sight.

Questions

We have tried to grasp the significance of a philosophical paragraph concerning the structure of belief in others. Which of your questions are not answered? In particular, regarding that structure, what might you disagree with? Further, in regard to some of the comments about the structure, what questions do you have? Why might you disagree?

'Proportion' as the Pilgrim has used it, means that to the extent one thing is not the case, another thing will be. Can I describe any experience in life from which I have learned this?

The 'human basics' or Culture, Environment, Experience and Expectations (CE4 or See-Level) refer to various scientific avenues to deepened understanding of existential difference. Do I see the difference of those avenues to understanding from a more philosphical avenue? Do those avenues help or hinder my understanding of the structure of belief in others? How?

Leaving un-differentiation can go wrong; we have only to turn to the media to know that. However, to the extent that leaving un-differentiation means not identifying, that is, believing in and loving others, why should it be less likely to go wrong?

The sense of the structure of belief in others is union in difference. Aiming for that goal requires the sixth member of the structure of belief in others. Why is not identifying self or others with 'satisfaction and assurances' integral to that aim?

Having expectations and identifying oneself or others with them are not the same things. To identify oneself is to conform to others' rules of thought and action. The hallmark of such conformity is not that it is right but rather that it satisfies and/or assures others. Likewise, to identify others is to expect their conformity with one's own or one's group expectations merely for the sake of the satisfactions and/or assurances one gets from such conformity. As parent or teacher or friend or lover or spouse or member of a particular group, do I recognize such identification? In others? In myself?

Franz Kafka is reported to have said that the sense of life is that it ends. Only that? Or is the sense of life discovered by the recognition of our poverty, as Certeau suggests? Then, what can be said of the way to that end?

Notes

1. Donnelly, Dody, *Team*, New York, Paulist, 1977.
2. Nussbaum, Abraham, 'The Faith of a Doctor,' *Commonweal*, 6 April 2007.
3. *L'étranger*, 224. The passage: '*Certes, là où n'y a pas union, la différence est inerte; elle n'est plus le ferment du sens. Mais l'union devient stérile et insignifcante si elle ne renait plus de la difference qui la met en question.*'
4. Mayeroff, Milton, *On Caring*, New York, Harper and Row, 1971.
5. Brooks, David, 'Battle of Narratives in Mideast.' In *The Denver Post*, 10 March 2007.
6. Rilke, Rainer Maria, *Letters to a Young Poet*, New York, W. W. Norton, 1954.

Chapter 4

Jesus, Believer in Others

Yet God became as humans are.
　　　Paul of Tarsus, Letter to the Philippians

So great a difference between humans and God!
　　　Augustine of Hippo, On the Trinity

What does one really do when one believes in others and lives along the questions? What fits well with not identifying; that is, with believing love? The Pilgrim's imaginative answer is found in what he lets us 'see' in Jesus. Jesus questions, Jesus evokes questions, Jesus is a question. In *The Stranger,* Certeau finds in the Gospel of John a 'thread of gold', a priceless representation of Jesus, whom he freely contemplates and interprets for his reader. What Certeau suggests we see in Jesus leads surprisingly to things we can say about the Other, God.

Contemplation

One way we contemplate is when we are deeply involved in the observation of someone's words and deeds. Contemplation is like the imaginative activity of the careful painter or film director. It is seeing and hearing an other who is here or elsewhere, who is now or then. When an other is elsewhere and elsewhen, using our imagination, we can still sense them, and we can still make them present to our understanding. In this case what we need are written (or visual) representations; such as what we have in writing in the New Testament Gospels. Contemplation by means of images drawn with words on pages may be as effective for understanding as when an other is actually here before us.

Much of what we are able to think or understand about an other represented to us pictorially or in writing depends upon the additional knowledge which we bring to the representation. From the beginning, the faithful have seen and heard Jesus in terms of the culture or habits of their own day. At Rome in about AD 300 Christ was imagined in a catacomb fresco as a beardless Roman shepherd, a lamb upon his shoulders; in Constantinople (modern Istanbul) he was imagined in icons with an emphasis upon colours, exemplifying the ideas of ancient Christian writers, for example, wearing white at the Transfiguration. We too can observe him in our terms, such as those of the modern scientific culture of our day.

There is a risk in bringing our CE4, our ideas to contemplation or interpretation of gospel images of Jesus; it lies in the fact that those who contemplate may see no more than what they merely wish or have been told to see. The risk is lessened to the extent that what is attributed to the observed subject is authentically human and does justice to what authors of the Gospels certainly wished to say. To the extent that the New Testament is an effect of its authors' contemplation of Jesus, it is about their CE4, how they observed Jesus according to the things they remembered and/or had heard about him and according to how in their day they thought about those things. In the contemplation of Jesus sketched in *The Stranger*, the Pilgrim carefully respects what the New Testament author John re-presents. In this way our Guide avoids having us create a merely contemporary portrait; he respects as far as possible an ancient verbal representation of Jesus not only as other but also as Other. Certeau lets us bring to John's verbal images of Jesus not only an understanding of the structure of belief in others but also additional elaborations of our own, consistent with that structure and with Scripture. He makes room for the expression of one's difference, all that one brings to a scene, and perhaps of one's desire in relation to an other.

Psychological qualities of a believer in others

The thinking of one modern psychologist allows us to add to how we think of a relation of belief or trust in others. We are given qualities or attributes to add to the Pilgrim's own contemplation of Jesus, thereby enhancing an image of Jesus as a believer in others.

Dr Murray Bowen, MD (1913–1993) was an existential psychologist, a professor of psychiatry and developer of an effective path toward healing un-differentiation in relationships, especially, but not solely, in the family. His ideas about human emotional functioning were comprehensively summarized some years ago by Michael E. Kerr in an issue of *The Atlantic* magazine.[1] Bowen's ideas on the well-defined self fit well with the Pilgrim's on the subjective structure of belief. When Bowen speaks of an 'inner directed adult', a 'differentiated' or 'well-defined self', it is easy to see that what he says applies to Jesus as Certeau contemplates him. A differentiated way of behaving indicates a differentiated way of thinking. That is, as Kerr informs us, for Bowen 'differentiation is a product of a way of thinking'. A way of thinking is evident in a way of behaving.

Here, closely following Kerr's summary, is a listing of differentiated, inner directed behaviours observed in adults, more in some than in others but to one extent or another in many if not most. While always sure of their beliefs and convictions, well-differentiated adults are not dogmatic or fixed in their thinking. They listen without reacting and communicate without antagonizing others. They are secure within themselves, and their functioning is not affected by praise or criticism. They can respect the identity of an other without becoming critical or emotionally involved in trying to modify that person's life course. They are realistically aware of their dependence on their fellows and are free to enjoy relationships. They do not have a 'need' for or excessive dependence upon others that can impair functioning; others do not feel used by them. Tolerant and respectful of difference, they are not prone to engage in polarized debates, they are realistic in their assessments of themselves and of others and are not pre-occupied with their place in a hierarchy.[2]

Bowen lists one other noteworthy characteristic: a high degree of 'emotional neutrality'. That is, those who leave undifferentiation are to a degree separate, detached, different – not only in their bodies and minds but especially in their emotions. Thus, we can see why Jesus would not identify himself or others with emotionally tinged needs for satisfactions and assurances. This does not mean that he had no emotion or passion and never expressed it; it means an easy self-control. As Certeau might say of Jesus, using Kerr's words for Bowen's thinking, 'He tolerates intense feelings well, and so he does not act automatically to alleviate them. His level of chronic anxiety (which is fearing what might be rather than what is) remains very low, and he can adapt under most stresses without developing symptoms.'[3]

As we shall see, emotional neutrality is made manifest in Jesus' respect for difference, not only that of others but also his own. Jesus seems to exhibit to a great extent the ability to differentiate oneself 'without being emotionally invested in one's own viewpoint or in changing the viewpoints of others'.[4] His caring was moved not by his own, but rather by others' need. Everyone takes positions in relation to others, but not everyone is emotionally neutral to the degree of Bowen's well-differentiated self.

Thus Bowen, through Kerr's listing, allows us to suppose compatible psychological refinements to how Certeau sees and hears Jesus with others. It is a list of what humans are capable of. It is not a list drawn from wishful thinking, it is a list based on careful, documented observation and measurement of human behaviour through the lens of differentiation. As will be seen, a contemplation of Jesus as a believer in others is compatible with Bowen's observation of the behaviours of a differentiated person. Believing in others, Jesus not only models not identifying oneself and others with selfish expectations but also the differentiated behaviour and thinking of a well-defined, 'inner directed, adult'. Jesus' belief in others is as unconditional as his identity is differentiated. He goes to his death by refusing every kind of social isolation or non-existence.

Contemplating the human difference of Jesus

As Certeau contemplates certain scenes in the Gospel of John, it is obviously human behaviour which he observes. As a Christian, John accepts Jesus' identification with something wholly Other. Here, however, that fact is beside the point. To be confessed as truly divine, Jesus has also to be recognized as truly human.

In *The Stranger*, Certeau writes at length about what he sees and hears in three scenes in John's Gospel. On the one hand, each instance discloses Jesus as a well-differentiated adult, a believer in others. On the other hand, Jesus is disclosed affecting others as we would expect such a person to affect them. They discover unexpected choices. To the extent that Certeau sees and hears Jesus as authentically, wholly, human, he contemplates what John clearly had in mind. For example:

With a Samaritan woman (John 4:5–30; 39–42)

Meeting a Samaritan woman at a well, Jesus asks her for a drink. She says, 'What? You are a Jew, and you ask me, a Samaritan, for a drink?' Because, as John adds, 'Jews, in fact, do not associate with Samaritans.' But Jesus resists her identification of him with what she knows of the Jews of her day. Jesus refuses to be 'placed'; he maintains his difference from an other's expectations of him. In Certeau's words, 'He is of course a Jew: by his culture, by his docility to the *Law* [the six collections of texts forming the major portion of the Hebrew Bible], but he is not identifiable with any of that. He suggests something else, critical of the absolute represented by this racial condition: he is someone who exists ...'⁵

Jesus is not identifiable, not known merely because he conforms to standards of a particular group. He differentiates himself from expectations formed in the woman's past contact with Jews who were hostile to Samaritans. He is a Jew, but his position is different from that of any other Jew. Something about him attracts, does not repel, this woman.

Throughout her conversation with Jesus, she recognizes his as well as her own different existence. In relation to him, it becomes possible for her to recognize something about herself – she says, 'I have no husband.' Jesus replies, 'You are right to say that.' Their dialogue takes them into her life. Out of their interaction she begins to discern new possibilities for her future. She wonders 'whether he is the Christ'. She hurries to tell others about this different Jew who has told her 'everything she ever did'.

The episode of the man healed of blindness (John 9)

Here we look at what Certeau sees in John's story of several related encounters. Briefly, the story begins with an encounter of a man with Jesus who heals the man's blindness. The story moves through encounters of the Pharisees with the man and his parents; in these encounters the Pharisees express their exclusive, self-isolating attitude towards the man and towards Jesus. The story concludes with the man once more encountering Jesus. The man and the Pharisees illustrate in distinctive ways the effect of Jesus' differentiated belief or trust upon other liberties. The two ways are distinguished by their outcomes.

It is the Pharisees who comment on Jesus' resistance to their wish to have him conform with what they hold is the meaning of the *Law*. Jesus differentiates himself from their expectations; he anoints a beggarly man. From the start the Pharisees deny their poverty; they do not believe in him. They will not even ask a simple question, Could this man be of God? Instead, they only believe that, by healing on the

Sabbath, 'This man cannot be of God, he does not keep the Sabbath.' They are hostile. They doubt what knowing witnesses tell them. They say to the beggar's parents, 'Is this man really your son who you say was born blind?' The hard liners are represented as unable to entertain a possibility contrary to their received ideas. Their position is fixed, isolated from others' questions, and so it is inert; they cannot make room for a difference, Jesus, who brings their union to a test. They discover no sense in their poverty, for they do not recognize it. They can see no choices other than those which their expectations allow them to see.

Others are not so closed, and so they are willing to face the questions which a difference, a liberty, brings into their midst. While some say, 'He is possessed', others say, 'These are not the words of a man possessed' (John 10:23). The man healed of his blindness knows his position. He was blind, now he is not. He will not change his story, even if the Pharisees wish to eliminate what he says by intimidating him. Like Jesus, he differentiates himself from the expectations of the Pharisees. So that, by the end of the story, he is offered a chance to respond to Jesus asking, 'Do you believe in the Son of Man?' That is, Do you believe in me?

Thus, an unforeseen, surprising question opens a door to a possible, different future and to the discernment of other, yet unforeseen choices. The man welcomes unexpected choices; the Pharisees do not.

Jesus before the Roman governor, Pontius Pilate (John 18 and 19)

Jesus resists, at times silently. During the hours preceding his crucifixion he maintains a position which lets him be identified neither with the Pharisees' nor with Pilate's expectations. At other times Jesus differs from Pilate even about the questions he should answer. Pilate asks, 'What have you done?' Certeau points out that, as is often the case in John's Gospel, Jesus' replies seem equivocal, beside the point. Thus, Jesus answers Pilate, 'Mine is not a kingdom of this world.' What kind of king is he then? In Pilate's world, where one comes from speaks of who one is and of what one can do. Pilate is a Roman official, therefore, backed by the power of Rome, he stands assured of what he is and can do. Jesus resists Pilate by bringing Pilate's assumption into question. Is Roman citizenship all there can be to who one is and to what one can do? In his role as judge, Pilate is invited to look deeper into the origins of his own existence.

Following the trend of Jesus' question and trying to find a way out of his predicament with the crowd, Pilate asks Jesus, 'Where did you come from?' Jesus is guilty of no violation of Roman law, but Pilate is afraid to uphold it. He wants Jesus to place himself in relation to Jewish law, to say anything to show he has broken some law. Jesus says nothing, he does not identify with Pilate's fearful wish to find an easy way to a choice which Pilate knows is wrong: the condemnation of Jesus. Jesus silently respects Pilate's liberty; Jesus resists Pilate's wish to have Jesus judge himself and thereby to give Pilate a way to escape the burden of having to exercize that liberty.

As is well known, Pilate then goes with a perverse choice (he hands Jesus over to the military) for no reason other than that he is afraid of trouble with the Jewish leaders. Like the Pharisees with the man healed of blindness, Pilate denies his poverty, does not believe in Jesus and so in this instance discovers no sense to that poverty. Pilate is different from the priests to the extent that he seems to have glimpsed a choice. Perhaps, more than they, he is blameworthy. Anyway, he recedes into sterile identification with the coarse union specified by the expectations of the crowd incited by the priests.

Jesus' effect upon others

As we have noted, in the cases of Pilate and of the Pharisees and in the cases of the man born blind and of the Samaritan, we see two outcomes in the typical pattern of Jesus' encounters with others. Typically Jesus evokes awareness of choices based upon a recognition of the poverty of ones's knowledge. On the one hand, Pilate and the Pharisees join to a denial of poverty a denial of any union with a quickening difference; their encounters with Jesus end with a choice of deadening isolation, of conformity with the agreements of a closed group. On the other hand, the man healed of blindness and the Samaritan woman move towards a union quickened by a difference, the register of their perception has changed, they have seen a possible different path forward. What do we discern leading up to those new paths?

Encountering Jesus, some trust him in return for his trusting them. Thus, recognizing their poverty and mutual existence, they are ready to listen, to question their own difference and to face unforeseen choices. We see that pattern clearly in the case of the Samaritan woman and the blind man. It is noteworthy that each is a member of a less powerful minority. Conformity with expectations which they had no part in making seems less attractive than its opposite; differentiation in the face of those expectations.

The woman's change of mind, her recognizing the sense of her poverty, happens in stages. First, her preconception of Jews becomes a question. Jesus' words and deeds do not conform with what she has learned about and so expects of Jews. Next she finds her identification of herself leading to a liberating question. Jesus tells her, 'You are right to say, "I have no husband".' From there she recognizes in a new way everything she has ever done. Finally, she recognizes that this different Jew has turned Jewish hopes (shared by the Samaritans) into another question: she wonders, 'Could he be the Christ?' What life choices could an affirmative answer to that bring her?

In his own encounter with the Pharisees, the man healed of blindness takes steps toward a greater recognition of his own different existence. In response to the Pharisees who 'did not want to believe' in the man's healed vision, the man is 'simply faithful to a fact'. As Certeau continues, 'The efforts his judges make to convince him of falsehood are precisely what lead him to reflect. Little by little he discerns in a gesture (his anointing by Jesus) its sense, and in an act its author.'[6] The Pharisees, in effect, further the impact of Jesus upon the poor man. Having had to question his own difference, he is last seen with Jesus. There he confirms his steps toward unforeseeable choices. He says to Jesus, 'Lord, I believe you are the Son of Man.' From there, what will be the extent of the man's identifying himself and others? Can we imagine that such identification will increase or decrease?

In the cases of the Samaritan woman and of the man born blind, differentiation leads to sense, a union in difference with Jesus who always manages to elude others' grasp until the time he chooses. What is more, in Jesus' encounters with the woman and the beggar, we hear no dogmatism. He listens without antagonism; he is not emotionally involved in trying to change either of them.

In the case of powerful majorities, the effect of encounter with Jesus is ultimately different: They too are invited to belief in an other and, as a consequence, to question their own difference or lack of it, and so they come to the brink of unforeseen choices. But they deny their basic human poverty. The grip of the need for conformity with a dominant Jewish or Roman group is also irresistible. So we see Pharisees and Pilate refuse an invitation and step back from different, potentially self-differentiating choices. In the end we see no sense in their encounter with the other, no union in difference with Jesus, but rather his mortal exclusion.

The Pharisees 'did not want to believe'. Not in the man healed by Jesus and not in Jesus himself. As John tells us, 'They did not want to believe that this man born blind had recovered his sight.' The man's insistence upon what he knows forces the Pharisees into having to choose between believing him or believing their assumption that Jesus is a sinner. So, unwilling to face the questions the facts pose, they drive away the man who now sees. With their gesture they isolate themselves from Jesus as well as from the man.

Jesus' resistance-existence brings the religious and political leaders face-to-face with their own existence and with what they claim to be true. In regard to Pilate, Certeau observes,

'Unlike the leaders of the Jews who were exploiting the power of the Roman Governor, Jesus recognizes the Roman governor's authority. He responds to him as a judge with a right to interrogate him.'[7] We know Jesus' last hours were ones likely to evoke many emotions, yet he does not allow them to influence his response to an other.

Jesus believes in Pilate, respects his liberty; he is not emotionally invested in his own viewpoint or in changing the viewpoint of Pilate (or any of the others). Jesus gives Pilate no reason to react let alone to condemn, but he does give Pilate reason to question his own conscience and to face hard choices. Pilate almost believes in Jesus, but in the end he betrays that belief and justice, the reason for his power. He refuses to affirm his incapacity to know this other and allows Jesus to be identified by expectations satisfying and assuring to the priests. As Roman governor, he betrays his conscience. He settles more or less for undifferentiated union with the party who want Jesus dead. Like the Jewish leaders, instead of moving towards union in difference, Pilate moves towards self-serving identification with what the leaders expect, towards isolating Jesus.

Finally, Jesus' behaviour towards Pilate is like that towards the woman and towards the beggar. There is no dogmatism, antagonism or emotional attempt to change Pilate. Furthermore, Jesus' awareness of dependence upon Pilate is clear. Clear too is the absence of polarized debate. Certainly, there is in John's representation no evidence of Jesus' preoccupation with maintaining a position in society.

At the start we supposed Jesus' manner or way of proceeding to be that of one who, at least to some extent, believes in others. We therefore supposed that he is one who takes union in difference as the sense of belief. That is, in some records of Jesus' dialogue with others, we have seen the following patterns. First, in regard to Jesus himself, we see that he resists identifying and being identified by others. By that kind of resistance, he invites others' recognition of their poverty and belief in him. Also, he exhibits behaviours and thinking of a 'differentiated self' within his society. A differentiated way of behaving indicates a differentiated way of thinking. A poverty funds that way of thinking. Thus, he tends to the sense of human existence, union in difference.

In regard to Jesus as others encounter him we see that they are brought in effect to points which include the necessity of recognition or denial of their poverty but without emotional pressure from Jesus; a return to themselves with a question about their identification of Jesus and of themselves; and, depending upon their answer to that question, radically different outcomes regarding their future with others.

Belief in others funds faith in God

We come to the confession or recognition behind faith. Up to this point we have been meditating upon the structure of belief or trust in others. We have been looking through the lens of the philosophical language of the Pilgrim and the psychological language of Murray Bowen. We have contemplated belief in others in encounters retold in the Gospel of John. We have elaborated some implications by contemplating or carefully observing Jesus in encounters with others. How does the understanding of human belief in others help us understand the structure of faith or trust in the Other, God?

Speaking philosophically, John's representation of Jesus' encounters with others do not let us see anything different from the kind of thing we can see by contemplating Socrates as Plato represents him. From this point of view, contemplation gives us a sort of portrait. Socrates too seems to have been a well-differentiated member of his society. Records of Buddha or Muhammad might also disclose their having had effects upon others comparable to the effects of Jesus or Socrates. In encounters with any of those figures, others had to choose to recognize their incapacity to know them and thus to begin to believe them.

On the other hand, in *The Stranger*, Certeau thinks and contemplates not only as a philosopher but also as a Christian theologian. He writes as one of those who, inspired by puzzling reality and by the Gospels, answers two questions[8] radically affecting existence. He includes himself among those who answer those questions, confessing: 'You are the Christ' and 'You know that I love you.' Then what contemplation yields is not only a human portrait but also an image of the Divine. Together, those create a holy icon. That is, for Christians, an other, Jesus, is simultaneously the Other. So, we see that belief in the Other, not wanting to be without the Other, is where desire for union takes someone like Thérèse de Lisieux who believes because she wants no thing but rather wants that Other.

This brings us once again to the paragraph we are studying. Here I have altered it to read as we can now see clearly the second discourse must be read.

> When we confess our incapacity to know the Other, we confess simultaneously the Other's existence, our own (to which we are returned) and a fundamental reciprocity between us. To the extent we *agree not to identify with anything the Other can expect from us and not to identify the Other with satisfactions or promises we hope to take from the Other*, we discover the sense of the *poverty* which funds all communication. This poverty signifies in effect both the desire which ties us to and the difference which separates us from the Other. That is the structure of faith in God.

From recognition of our poverty to not identifying, all the members we have been taking note of in the structure of belief in others are members of the structure of faith in God. The structures are the same. Nevertheless, we can ask: Are 'belief' and 'faith' the same as or only like each other and, if like, what is their difference? Furthermore, what, if anything, can we say about God?

'Faith ...'
From the point of view of our study of the Pilgrim's paragraph, faith or trust in God must be the same as belief in others; at least to the extent that faith is not possible without its foundation in human existence. Faith like belief begins and ends with our human incapacity to know the unknown. That

is, as suggested by Certeau, the faith in God of which theologians speak is a 'modality' of human belief in others. Faith, in the theological sense, must affirm whatever can be known about the structure of belief in its philosophical sense. Theologically, faith is differentiated from belief by the grace or 'self-communication'[9] of God to humans. Just as Christian love or charity is a modality of human love, so too Christian faith in God is a modality of human belief in others. Theologians tell us that God's gift or grace enhances belief so that we can speak of faith, but not without supposing its human foundation.

What else does the Pilgrim have to say about believing in others which sheds light on faith? In a study he made, possibly as a preliminary step toward writing a book on human believing,[10] the Pilgrim suggests a simple but helpful image. Belief in others can be represented by what we do in daily life as a result of promises or assurances made to us.

Thus, for example, belief in an other happens when one decisively agrees to 'good news' from a credit card company. An employee of the company, a stranger, communicates a company promise. Certain minimum preconditions are deemed necessary for the promise to be fulfilled. To the extent that one conforms to those expectations, then, all one's getting and spending will be covered by the card company or by whomever it represents.

Like that, faith in God happens when one decisively agrees to some good news. For Christians that means the news that the Other, on behalf of whom John writes his Gospel, will fulfil a promise. The promise is that, to the extent that one performs a certain minimum precondition (love of the Other and of others), one is even now, and in the future shall be, rewarded. What more can be said about belief and its modality, faith?

Both modes of believing are structurally the same, both connote trust (one in others, one in the Other), and both have the same sense. Faith as well as belief begin and end with the unknown. In the relation of oneself to the Other who is God, one recognizes one's poverty and existence (one's own as well as the Other's) and an inevitable reciprocity including a proportional equality in liberty together with the desire for union and the necessity of difference. The sense of faith is the same as that of belief: union in difference.

Belief and faith are different to the extent that the subjects of the necessary practices are different. In the first case, both those who make and those who accept a promise of ultimate satisfaction are humans. In the second case, those who accept are also humans but, for Christians at least, the Other (Jesus Christ) who makes the promise of ultimate satisfaction is wholly Divine as well as wholly human. A great difference.

Belief and faith are also different because, as the Pilgrim points out, Christians understand that the fulfilment of God's promise is both already and not yet. As Christians hold, according to an ancient hymn, found today in Christian services, 'Christ has died, Christ is risen, Christ will come again.'

More importantly, belief and faith are different because, as in the example, belief in a creditor is contractual, subject to legal sanctions. Different subjects mutually agree to have their expectations controlled by objective rules (of a state and of a company). However, in the case of faith, the mutual agreement of subjects is understood as a covenant[11] (something more like love in a relationship between true friends – neither is likely to renounce it). Then liberties or differences agree to identify neither themselves nor the others with expected satisfactions and assurances; that is, both believers and the Other agree to act according to a faith and a charity expressive of mutually uniting desire and of separating difference. That is, as the first commandment implies, to whatever extent they are able, the faithful will expect no strange or foreign 'gods', no satisfactions and assurances, either for or from the Other. In other words, as far as possible faith like belief (a modality of love) is unconditional.

Remembering that in every relationship we are always to some extent unknown, that is, strangers to each other (even when we have known an other all our lives), we can now say that our belief in others exists to the extent that we recognize what is hidden, unknown in all our intercourse with them; to the extent that we recognize that they too exist as liberties united to and separated from others by desire and difference; and to the extent that we agree to identify neither ourselves nor them with anything that can be expected. Likewise, we can now say faith in God exists to the extent that a certain unconditionality is true of one's relation to the Other. Finally, we can say that to the extent that we actively discover the sense of belief in others, we actively discover the sense of Faith in the Other.

'God ...'

In our study of the Pilgrim's discourse, it is now that we come to where his thinking about faith might take us in regard to approaching the question of the Other's existence. First we consider that, since the time of Aristotle if not before, philosophers and theologians have tried to give logical arguments to show the Other, God, exists. At times those are called proofs. What they 'prove' is that it is possible God exists. One such argument, popular today, is the so-called argument from design. Its logic is this:

> Every design has a designer.
> In nature we find design.
> Design in nature has a designer.

The argument is unconvincing not only because it leaves unanswered the question of our incapacity to know; it assumes we know all there is to know about apparent design in nature. Why must a design in nature have a designer? The 'proof' in the three logical lines may too easily feed an illusion that its words give us anything more than words about a supposed designer. Paradoxically, certainty about knowing God exists would seem to contradict Faith based upon recognition of human incapacity to know the other.

Another argument for the existence of God also dates back to Plato and Aristotle. It is discussed in writer-authorities like

Thomas Aquinas and his followers down to today. It is an argument from cause:

> Every thing which exists has a cause.
> The whole universe exists.
> The whole universe has a cause.

Again left unanswered is the question of our incapacity to know; it is assumed we know all there is to be known about causation in nature. Once more one can question what the conclusion gives of the Other and whether it might engender a false sense of certainty opposed to the recognized poverty of belief and so of faith.

It is tempting to construct a similar argument following Certeau. It might go something like this:

> No thing is without an other.
> The universe is.
> The universe is not without an Other

This logical argument is valid to the same extent as the two previous arguments. Like the others it too can be taken to postulate a relevant hypothesis (God exists) and asks for a way to verify it. But before we see how it might be verified, we can consider ways to approach the God question other than purely logical ones.

One might ask, What was there before the 'Big Bang'? Pope John Paul II cautioned against such an inquiry, likening such an inquiry to trying to know the mind of God. From their point of view, some scientists say that the question about before such a thing as the Big Bang is meaningless. Nevertheless, in *Thinking about God* (1975), John Macquarrie points to examples of questions which are similar in that they must bring us to the border of known with the unknown. While they do not answer, they surely 'lead us into the question of God'.

The question of God may arise along with one's simple, some might say surprising or shocking, experience of wonder at being in the world at all. Then too, in a distracting, technologically sophisticated culture, a question which may too easily go undiscovered is: Why is there something rather than nothing? That is, as Macquarrie puts it more specifically, Why is there 'an ordered world, capable of being rendered intelligible to the intelligences that it has itself brought forth, rather than an unknowing and unknown chaos'? Another question leading to the question of God is moral: Why ought we to do anything at all, and what is the sense of 'oughtness' or moral obligation? Along with logical 'proofs' of God's existence one may wonder about what such things tell us.

Macquarrie also points to the question of meaning or sense, a question which seems most compatible with the way the Pilgrim is showing us. Macquarrie writes, 'We live all the time in various contexts of meaning (which) give direction or purpose to whatever we are doing.' Such a question leads to the question of an over-arching context of meaning and so goes to the question of God which our Guide opens. In response to an interviewer who asked her what she thought about 'God', the film actress Katharine Hepburn replied, 'I can't figure it.' That is, she was saying, I can't say what sense it has. From our point of view, speaking of 'God' assumes or postulates that something exists and, as Hepburn affirms, 'it' resists our grasp. Probably without realizing it, she was saying, 'Whatever the word "God" refers to resists my capacity to know or contain it.' Recognizing her incapacity to grasp that Other, she was simultaneously recognizing the Other's existence. In other words, she was on the verge of the discovery of the 'context of meaning' which belief in others suggests and, in that context a particular direction or purpose: union in difference. Then, if she wanted, she was inaugurating a search at least like that of the Samaritan woman, if not like that of Thérèse de Lisieux. In other words, as the Pilgrim says in the Italian version of *The Stranger*,[12] two searches are articulated: 'To know their world, the faithful must indeed know the Master intimately, but the reverse is equally true.'

Some might ask: Isn't virtual faith such as Hepburn's merely the effect of wishful thinking? Not, it seems, in her case. She indicates nothing about wishes and fears and so is not speaking from the position suggested by Freud who understands religion as a relation with an Other, which is as an 'illusion', like that of a literal 'rapture', generated in the imagination to protect us from the natural uncertainty surrounding existential satisfactions and assurances. Whatever the truth in Freud's view of the psychology of religious belief, a relation of belief or trust in the Other cannot be reduced to being no more than what Freud suggests may be true in terms of human psychology. To the extent that Hepburn is speaking existentially of the human desire to know the unknown, her response includes identifying neither herself nor the Unknown with any expected satisfactions and assurances. There is no illusion; rather there is opening to the 'indifference' or detachment of a purified human desire or longing.

Augustine says, 'My love is my weight.' A great enough weight along with a pulley can put a thing in motion. Like the weight in a clock, the 'weight' or principle of the Pilgrim's structure of belief or faith is the unknown. It moves one to questioning. To the extent that the existence of God is uncertain, the Pilgrim's philosophical point of view permits agreement with those who say that God's existence is a hypothesis. Then the 'God hypothesis' gives to those who answer Jesus' two questions an existential basis. To the extent that they believe in or love others, they confess simultaneously God's existence and their desire for union.

A more scriptural (and therefore more theological) point of view suggests a verifiable prediction which, to the extent that it is fulfilled, will verify, will show the hypothesis to be true. In John's Gospel, Jesus says that his followers are to be known by their love of others. To the extent that those who respond to Jesus' questions of belief and love believe in and love others, they confess Jesus' existence in a way which can be verified. That the Other exists is demonstrated to the extent that others see love, good done – especially to strange or different, perhaps hostile liberties. Contemplating such love of others invites us to confess that the Other exists not only hypothetically but also actually. There is the test by which the 'God hypothesis' is shown to be true. There is a way to the to the conclusion that God exists. To the extent that love is made visible by what is done to others, we can say that God (who, as the New Testament letter of John tells us, is Love[13]) exists.

Towards the end of the Gospel of John are these words: 'This disciple is the one who vouches for these things and has written them down, and we know that his testimony is true.' 'We' is written there because it is a community of faithful which affirms what the writer of the Gospel witnessed. That is, the recipients of John's words recognize the Other whom they have no capacity to know other than by what is being expressed, not only in word but also especially in deed.

The author of the Gospel tells us what he has seen. In the last sentence of the Gospel, John recognizes his own poverty, the incapacity to know and therefore to express, which funds the desire and the difference which his Gospel signifies: 'There are many other things that Jesus did; if all were written down, the world itself, I suppose, would not hold all the books that would have to be written.'

Thus, according to our reading of Certeau, it is resistant-existent others who ever invite recognition of the Other. That is true globally. It is also true for Christians who recognize in the other, Jesus. Then their belief becomes faith in an other, Jesus, who is simultaneously the Other, and its sense is union in difference. For the Pilgrim, seeking to understand the global structure of belief in others means seeking to understand the structure of faith in the Other, God. As Thérèse de Lisieux, the Little Flower, puts it, 'I believe because I want to.' Taking this enigmatic figure's existential recognition of want as her confession of Christian poverty and desire, verified in the example of her life, we can say she wants nothing more nor less than the Other, without whom it would not be possible for her to live anymore.[14]

By now the meaning of not identifying the Other, God, with satisfactions and assurances, may be clear. Christians commit themselves to love others and the Other for themselves and not for anything they can expect to gain from either of them. Likewise, the meaning of not identifying themselves with anything God might expect may also be clear. Christians recognize that God wants their faith and charity. And yet, although the effect of faith and charity, good done as well as goods given to others, is existentially important, even necessary, in a relation to the Other such things can't be substituted for one's desire for the Other. God will not be bought. Besides, as the Pilgrim reminds us, we go finally to God not only as we were born, naked, but also denuded.

The difference of Jesus is the difference of God

To the extent that Christians have faith in others, they have faith in Jesus the Other, represented for them in every human other whom they meet; they have faith in God. Much of what Certeau's paragraph permits fellow believers to say about global humanity (summed up in the existential structure of belief) can also be said of Jesus and must therefore be said of God. That way the faithful are following a rather simple traditional Christian rule. The rule is called the 'communication of properties or attributes'.[15] Today we might say that in a more understandable way by speaking of the communication of differentiated behaviours. What the rule means is that many of the things which can be attributed to the human difference Jesus can, and must be, attributed to the divine difference Jesus. What is referred to is a kind of translation or taking something from one side to another. For example, if it can be said that Jesus believes in or trusts others, the same can be said of God. And, if Jesus leaves others free, God leaves them free.

God, the Unknown, the Stranger

In *The Stranger*, the Pilgrim allows us to understand a number of things about God. In their worship, when Christians confess 'We believe in God', they confess their incapacity to know the Other who is not only different from but also more than anything which can be represented verbally or nonverbally. As a consequence, the faithful can say 'God exists.' As a further consequence, they say God is involved in human existence (to which they are returned). They say that God is not only different from but also desirous of human existence. At the beginning of *The Stranger*, Certeau writes,

> Every Christian, I believe, moves and works among others in the manner of the disciples ... making their way to the village of Emmaus with a stranger: So you know nothing of what happens here? You are not one of us! They had to share the same bread to recognize Jesus in him.[16]

The bread of the poor. After the Resurrection, for Christians it is daily the same as before. The ordinary experience of the faithful is this. Faith like belief begins and ends with recognition of the Unknown. With every stranger, the Unknown Other, the Misunderstood is known.

In their worship, besides confessing God's existence, Christians make another confession. Believers say, 'I confess, I have sinned, I have missed the mark.' That is, to the extent that I have identified others with idols, with hoped-for satisfactions or assurances (wealth or possessions) I have identified the Other with them; for, we are told, God is not to be identified with idols or other gods. Likewise, to the extent that I have identified myself with satisfactions and assurances which God might be said to expect, I have wandered away from a relation of faith and charity and its sense; for, as Psalm 51 says, 'Sacrifice gives You no pleasure, were I to offer holocaust, You would not have it.'

God, Union in Difference

Given the Covenant or partnership between God and humankind, believers also confess that God is the Other with whom they are mutually dependent and that God desires knowledge of or union with them. Christian believers bind themselves to live that dependence to the extent they can – with God's help. The reason is this. What Scripture and differentiated tradition tell Christians about God and what philosophy and science tell us about our humanity come together in the other/Other, Man-God, Jesus Christ. He is himself a union in difference: two different natures, human and divine, united in one 'person'. And, through others, we know him and so we know of another union in difference: that of Father, Son and Spirit, three different 'persons' in the Unity of the Unknown Other. God is Union in Difference.

Comes a Thief

As a very old Christian saying puts it, 'Comes a stranger, Christ comes.' Certeau writes that 'the Other always arrives from the unknown and as unknown ... like a thief.'[17] In other words, 'Comes a stranger, a thief comes.' Like a bag-snatch, the Other often takes us by surprise. For example, shocks in our lives, delivered by other liberties can be particular signs of the Other's presence. Not an idea which is likely to be our first in relation to those who in some sense take from us our certainties, our securities, our defences. However, why can it not be so? One arrives at an answer to that most easily by looking at consequences. To the extent that surprises by others tend to encourage our recognition of our poverty and to lessen our identifying ourselves and/or others with lost objects, who can say there is not something divine at work? In any event, Certeau would have believers be watchful for the thief in every encounter with an other. That may be so especially in those encounters which somehow shock, awakening sleepers to what they may have forgotten or do not want to see. After all, isn't a friend someone who tells us what we actually need to see, not what we mistakenly want to hear?

When the unexpected overtakes us, transforming an ordinary moment (like coming home or meeting a stranger) into a moment of shock ('Surprise! Happy Birthday!' or 'Go and call your husband') and altering what one may do next (couch and TV or friends and party? or 'Could this be the Christ?'). Or, when a true friend has told us what we need but do not want to see. Or, when we are surprised, shocked by what we hear others say or by what we see them do to us, robbing us of our securities or condemning us for our blindness, that is, when we are brought back to ourselves to question ourselves about ourselves. Or, when we realize that we must examine our expectations not only of ourselves but also of others. Those especially are moments in which the faithful, like all humans, returned to themselves, are able to recognize the stranger, the thief, the unreadable, perhaps hostile, liberty who surprises them along the way.

'I come like a thief.' This statement of Christ's in Revelations 16:25 echoes existential experience. With this image, the Pilgrim tells us what must be said of the Other. A thief is unknown. A thief is the stranger who is hidden, who takes us by surprise, and who disarms us. A thief makes us let go all our guarantees of safety and security, satisfactions and assurances. A thief is an unknown, perhaps hostile liberty, a difference who condemns us by showing us our lack of awareness of what we do not know. Paradoxically, a thief is someone we can believe because a thief reminds us of this truth: sooner or later we must finally surrender every satisfaction and assurance, for we shall die.

With the image of the thief, we avoid the easy mistake of making God an idol in the image of whatever things make us feel good about God. We avoid that mistake whenever what we say comes with our recognition of the limits or our know-ledge and of language: books to fill the world cannot grasp the Other. Whatever we say presupposes too that the Other is not the world; the stranger is a subject not some very big object, a subject for whom we need to have (to say the least) the utmost respect.

Interior Master

Finally, in *The Stranger*, as he does in an earlier writing,[18] Certeau reminds us of another touching scene from the Gospel of John. It is a reminder that Christians believe that Christ – unseen and yet nearby – makes the faithful aware of his presence through others, returning them to themselves and to the awareness that he is their own Interior Master. In the scene Martha, the sister of Mary (not Jesus' mother), welcomes Jesus to their home and then goes to call her sister. Speaking in a low voice, she says, 'The Master is here and wants to see you.'[19]

Questions

Do I think that a contemplation of Socrates as Plato tells us about him is different from a contemplation of Jesus as John tells us about him? Why?

Do I think Jesus' belief in others is somehow different from Buddha's? If I do, how do I reconcile that with the belief that Jesus is like us in all things (except only sin)?

Look at other accounts of Jesus with others. For example, at the meal given by Simon in his house (Luke 7:36–50) or in the Temple with an adulterous woman (John 8:2–11). Does Jesus appear to maintain a position based upon recognition of his own incapacity to know others? What do you see and hear in these stories which seems to confirm this? Do any of Jesus' words show him emotionally involved in changing others? How can the consequences of those encounters (with Simon, with the woman in Simon's house and with the woman in the Temple) be imagined as generally the same? At the end, do the others of those encounters with Jesus find themselves returned to themselves to ask questions leading to possible choices?

Is it true that faith in the Other, God, requires no proof or argument that God exists? How does the absence of a wholly convincing logical proof make faith more sincere, lessen the risk of making it somehow idolatrous?

Have I experiences which for me might illustrate the idea that Christ comes like a thief?

What happens when he have faith in God? What happens the moment Christians say, 'We believe in you, Father ...' What does our reading of Certeau allow us to think Christians confess in that moment?

Notes

1. Kerr, Michael E., 'Chronic Anxiety and Defining a Self', in *The Atlantic*, 8 September 1988, 35–58.
2. Ibid., 44.
3. Ibid., 46.
4. Ibid., 57.
5. *L'étranger*, p. 170.
6. Ibid., p. 234.
7. Ibid., p. 238.
8. See Mark 8:29 (with parallels) and John 21:15–17.
9. Rahner, Karl and Vorgrimler, Herbert, *Theological Dictionary*, New York, Seabury, 1973, 'Faith'.
10. Certeau, 'Croire: une pratique de la différence', Italy, Università di Urbino, Centro Internazionale di Semiotica e di Linguistica, *Documents de Travail*, 106, September 1981.
11. Rahner and Vorgrimler.
12. Certeau, *Mai senza l'altro*, Italy, Fabbri, 1997.
13. 1 John 4:8.
14. See John 6:67–9. The disciples believe, know, because of what they recognize.
15. Rahner, Vorgrimler, 'Communicatio Idiomatum'.
16. *L'étranger*, p. 9.
17. *L'étranger*, 2, pp. 225–45. The allusion is to Revelation 16:25.
18. Certeau, *Jean-Joseph Surin: Guide Spirituel*, France, Desclée de Brouwer, 1963, p. 33.
19. John 11:29.

Chapter 5

The Wisdom of Uncertainty

*Truly, Abba Joseph found the way, for he said,
'I do not know.'*
   from *Sayings of the Desert Fathers*

Speaking different languages

A first, philosophical reading of the paragraph repeated below gave us the global structure of human belief or trust in others. When we trust someone we implicitly recognize a certain ignorance of them, their and one's own different existence and a relationship between them and oneself. A second, theological reading of the paragraph gave us a particular reading of those same things including not only others but also the Other, God. We have begun to see reasons for two languages, one philosophical about what we learn in life from studying existence, another theological about what Christians bring to the same study from Scripture and their differentiated tradition. Central to the theological study is the fact that however 'faith' is taken, it implies a free choice. There is the starting point for a second, theological language. Then, for a Christian, a philosophical language of faith in others becomes a theological language of faith in the Other, Jesus Christ.

How are those languages related in the paragraph taken from Certeau's *The Stranger*? We start by recalling something Certeau observes in his book, cited earlier, *L'absent d l'histoire* (*The*

Absent from History). There, in chapter four on 'Mystical Language,' he reports on his study of the spiritual language of the fascinating seventeenth-century spiritual author Jean-Joseph Surin. One thing he looks at specifically is the relation between Surin's writings and the writing of John of the Cross. John's writing includes, on the one hand, his poetry and, on the other, his prose commentary on his poetry: one is not without the other. Though less evident, the same is true of Surin's writing. Of the complementary poetry and prose expressions, Certeau says that they signify by their separation one thing. He writes,

> Deux discors differents mais paralleles expriment, par leur écart meme (qui est 'proportion'), ce qu'aucun ne dit à lui seul ... Quoi qu'il en soit du détail de ce fonctionnement ... un même tropisme tourne ce prose vers le soliel de la poésie ...[1]

That is,

> Two different but parallel discourses express by their very separation (which is 'proportion') that which neither expresses by itself ... In every detail of this functioning ... the same search turns this prose toward the sun of poetry ...

Here then, for the last time, is the paragraph which has been guiding our inquiry.

> When we confess our incapacity to know others, we confess simultaneously their existence, our own (to which we are returned) and a fundamental reciprocity between them and us. To the extent we *agree not to identify with anything they can expect from us and not to identify them with satisfactions or promises we hope to take from them*, we discover the sense of the *poverty* which funds all communication. This poverty signifies in effect both the desire which ties us to others and the difference which separates us from them. The same is the structure of faith in God.

'Different but parallel discourses . . .'

If anything in that paragraph differentiates a second language or discourse (type of speech) from a first (of a different kind), it is its subjects. There are two: 'God . . .' and 'We . . .' The last proper noun in the paragraph is the subject which signifies a conversion or translation of the first discourse into the second. While the language of the first discourse expresses the existential structure of human belief in others, the language of the second expresses the existential structure of Christian (human) faith in the Other, God.

As we saw, our first reading is of a philosophical discourse. But can the discourse be the same if the other subject is divine? Is the discourse any longer philosophical? No, it is theological, inspired also by Scripture and differentiated tradition. A particular change in one subject inaugurates the differentiation or conversion of the reading of one paragraph into a reading of two discourses, forming together an ongoing union in difference. That conversion is inaugurated by a change in the reader. Just as, according to the Pilgrim, Jesus is the conversion of the Old Testament into the New, the reader like the writer, like Jacob wrestling with the angel, becomes the site of ongoing conversion or translation of the philosophical language of one discourse into the theological language of another, and vice versa.

It is Certeau who writes 'We'. Thereby he includes himself along with the other Christians for whom he writes. *The Stranger* begins, 'Every Christian, I believe . . .' The whole book is concerned with Christian faith in others and consequences. Just as the first discourse speaks for all humans, the second speaks for some humans – those who have freely made the choice to follow Jesus.

The two discourses are different. But are they parallel? That is, are they precisely similar? Certeau himself answers with the last sentence of the paragraph, 'The same is the structure of faith in God.' The similarity or parallel of the theological to the philosophical discourse lies in the fact that the human structure of belief in others and the structure of faith in the Other are the same. We remember too that belief and faith are not the same; they are modalities, similar but different modes of a relation. Thus, we see clearly that, for Certeau and for Christians, neither way of speaking, neither theological nor philosophical, is possible without the other; they form an on-going union in difference.

'Express by their very separation ...'
Given two languages or discourses (ways of speaking), we can ask: What do they 'express by their very separation (which is 'proportion') ... [and which] neither expresses by itself'? We recall first of all that what is between the different but parallel discourses is the 'same thing'. What then is this thing which is 'neither contained in a silence exterior to the text nor in a singular pronouncement'?

The sense of the structure discussed in each discourse is union in difference, humans with other humans and humans with the Other, God. That sense is discovered in an unending altering of one position or discourse by an other. There is an altering alternation like the one suggested by the image of Jacob and the angel at the brook of Jabbok. There is a to and fro, a struggle in which a subject is brought to one position and another, ever leaving open a space between them, a gap expressive of the same thing which neither says. As in the case of Jacob with the angel, there is no final reply to Jacob's request: 'Tell me your name.'[2] There is a 'not-said'.

'(Which is "proportion") ...'
Speaking theologically, in his treatise *On the Trinity* St Augustine exclaims, 'How great is the difference between humans and God!' Whatever is said of God can never be the same as what we say of humans; there is always the proviso: God is different. Never is everything said, always more is not-said. That not-said or 'unsayable' is what the gap between humans and God expresses. To the extent that words cannot fully express who an other or the Other is, only silence can fill the gap between discourses about the human and the divine. One may finally have to say along with Job answering God in the heart of the whirlwind, 'I had better lay my finger on my lips.'[3] Yet, even then one cannot stop wondering.

The expressive separation or gap between the two discourses is proportion, a relation of each discourse to the other. The proportion or relation which exists for each of them has ultimately to do with the differences of human and divine subjects. What separates, what is between them, is silence, a not-said referring to those subjective differences. What is obvious is that what can be expressed about human and divine subjects must ever be related as less to more. Even though what is not known, not said, about humans is unmeasurable, what is not said about the Other must be greater. If the whole world would not serve to contain what is not said about the human, Jesus, what could serve to contain what is not said about the divine? In other words there exists between the two discourses, a not-said, a proportion, for one a relation of less to more, for the Other a relation of more to less; for each a relation of union in difference.

Furthermore, as Certeau tells us in regard to the prose and poetic discourses of John of the Cross and of Jean-Joseph Surin, what is not expressed is 'localized neither in a silence exterior to the text' (that is, not in the mind of a receiver, a hearer or reader) 'nor in a singular pronouncement' (that is, by no authority, neither by John of the Cross nor by Surin, neither in poetry nor in prose; neither in theology nor in science, whether philosophical or modern).

There is always more to be known about others and the Other (and the world). That excess is what is not known and not-said by the gap, the separation or proportion created in the relationship of two different languages or types of discourse.

'The sun of poetry ...'
What is not expressed in either of those languages drives one who would try to express it toward another language. That is, as Certeau says in regard to John of the Cross and Surin, 'The same search turns ... prose toward the sun of poetry.' The search is for words with which to say what until a particular moment has remained unsaid; a seeker of words nibbles away at the unknown, resulting at times in something bright, like a 'sun', a recognition beginning and ending in a brilliant flash,

a union in difference, a linking of words and referent in some heretofore unexpressed manner. Here then is a message at least for the Christian theologian or philosopher. To the extent that either turns away from the sense of their 'same search', they miss the sense of what they profess; for to that extent they ignore both known and unknown, that is they abandon the relationship between them[4] and turn to merely repeating the past, seeking escape from the bright sun of poetry.

'Every detail of this functioning ...'
These are the details of how the gap or space (what is not said) functions have to do with its impact upon each discourse, each side of the relationship, the relation of each discourse to the other. The gap prevents any immediate and final reading of either discourse, as if there could ever be a time when no more could be said. Each discourse incessantly refers critically to the other; and that prevents the reduction of one or other to aesthetics (a consideration of what is better in creative expressions) or to morality (a consideration of what is better in expressive action). Arrival at the goal, any union of speech and reality, is given neither by one nor by the other discourse; it is not said.

With the creation of a space or gap, sense is fixed neither in one nor the other speech or discourse but rather 'between' them. Each discourse is symbolic in that neither is complete without the other. Like a union of different subjects, like (as St Paul tells us) Christ and his Church, these discourses are a union in difference. Thus, the symbolic inter-dependence or composition of different discourses becomes a kind of 'mystical style', indicating the secret or hidden, unknown or notsaid. The Pilgrim, in the two discourses, like John of the Cross in his, 'says what can't be said in a particular or placeable way, and thereby prevents the illusion of thinking that what one says is no different from, that it is identical with, what one is speaking of'. Thus it seems that, to the extent that philosophy and theology speak of the unspeakable, they do so finally by turning to metaphorical or figurative description, not of God but of experience.[5] Undeniably, something happens like what we hear of in the film *Paris, je t'aime*. A solitary woman from Denver in a Parisian park tells us that, while contemplating the lovely surroundings of nature, the city and children, she is overcome with an unforgettable sense which she can only describe as one of both sadness and joy. The source? Something deep from within? The Other?

No expressions can ever be adequate to others or the Other, God. Human believers in or lovers of the Other search endlessly for more. Two different relations, two different discourses exist. They each begin with a recognition of incapacity to grasp the other. They confess that the other/Other exists, is desirable – and finally, unspeakably different.

Long ago, St Augustine said as much in his *Confessions* when he wrote of what he and his mother Monica once experienced not long before her death. They were returning from Roman Milan to Roman North Africa. What they went through occurred in the garden of the house in which they stayed during a layover in Ostia, the seaport of Rome, at the mouth of the river Tiber.

There, he tells us, they conversed of the Unknown 'between ourselves', desiring and even briefly, he says, 'tasting' it. But then, he says, shortly 'we returned to the noise of language where every word is begun and ended'.[6] To the extent that limited words cannot express the Unknown, there can only be the noise of speech signifying in effect human diversity and longing.

In the conclusion of *The Mystic Fable*, Certeau gives an apt quotation from the twentieth-century French poet René Char. Char writes of poetic experience: '*En poésie, on n'habite que le lieu que l'on quitte, on ne crée que l'oeuvre dont on se détache, on n'obtient durée qu'en détruisant le temps.*'[7] That is, 'In poesy one inhabits no more than the place one leaves, one creates no more than the piece one lets go, one gains nothing lasting except by laying waste to time.' As good a description as any of the mystic (because hidden, known only by its effects) search to express things which defy capture in words.

How *The Stranger* functions in relation to the reader

We still have not answered every question about what distinguishes the two languages or discourses of the Pilgrim's dual paragraph. We found one answer in the different subjects and objects of the two discourses. (As a philosopher, one thinks about believing; as a theologian, one thinks about having faith.) Another answer lies in different readers.

The one paragraph text for *The Stranger* has a particular function in relation to the reader. To the extent that Certeau's way of thinking about existence interests the reader, it engages the reader's own desire and search for the not-said in union with a different author.

To the extent that a visitor to the text is engaged by it, the text functions in the following way. The *Spiritual Exercises* of St Ignatius of Loyola were composed in the early 1500s. Of that text Certeau writes,

> The text which thus articulates desire without taking its place does not work if it is not practiced by the other and if there is no Other. It depends upon the one to whom it is addressed and who is its beginning. What happens to such a text when the Other is lacking? The discourse is no more than an inert object if the visitor does not take a position, and if the Other is no more than a shadow. What remains is a tool marked only by vanished presences, if, outside it, there is no longer room for the *desire* which has organized it. It does not give as much as it presupposes. It is a literary space to which only the desire of an other gives sense.[8]

The 'other' to whom Certeau refers is the one who practices the *Exercises* with the guidance of Ignatius or with someone else adept at such guidance. The one who practices them is the one to whom they are addressed and the one who begins the journey through them, coming perhaps to an oasis or a 'taste' of union in difference (but one cannot stop there). And the *Exercises* will have no sense unless the visitor to them takes the position of one who desires the other. The Exercises begin and end there, with the desire for union in difference.

In other words, for a visitor to the text of *The Exercises* (and likewise, for a visitor to the text of *The Stranger*) there must be to some extent Augustine's weight or motivation. A basic question put before anyone who practices the *Exercises* or reads *The Stranger* is one of desire: 'What moves me?' or 'What do I want?' and 'Whom do I love?'

Our paragraph from *The Stranger* also works that way. It requires the engagement of the visitor; otherwise it is a dead letter. Like the Ignatian *Spiritual Exercises* Certeau's text ends where it begins: with that which each visiting liberty alone can bring, and with 'the desire which has organized it'; that is, a visitor to the text must finally decide to want what the text's author wanted when he wrote: the Other, the Stranger.

Certeau's text indicates a position globally in regard to others and particularly in regard to the Other. A search begins and ends when the visitor takes that position. The text of *The Stranger* gives new meaning to the expression, 'I don't know what I want.' But also, it allows it to be said: 'I do know that it is different from anything else.' Or as Certeau writes at the end of his book *Mystic Fable* (*La Fable Mystique*),

> Est mystique celui ou celle qui ne peut s'arrêter de marcher et qui, avec la certitude de ce qui lui manque, sait de chaque lieu e de chaque object que ce n'est *pas ça*, au'on ne peut résider *ici* ni se contente de *cela*.[9] (Certeau's emphasis)

That is,

> The mystic is she or he who can't stop moving and who, with the certainty of what they lack, knows of each place and of each object that it is *not that*, who knows that one cannot stop *there* or be satisfied with *that*.

In other words, the structure of belief or faith has also to do with accepting death; that is, with accepting the endless lack of satisfactions and assurances associated with the uncertainties of a way of belief in others. From that point of view, we are all mystics to the extent that we understand the final sense of our poverty. In the words of a modern monk of Athos, the Elder Joseph, to want to 'taste' what the Pilgrim calls union in difference, 'one has to be walking toward death at every moment'. The poverty we are born with is the poverty with which we die. Living a life by recognizing that poverty is what the dual paragraph is about. The Pilgrim articulates a way of 'standing in the question', a way of uncertainty, of putting into practice the saying of Maimonides a thousand years ago, 'Teach thy tongue to say, "I do not know" and thou shalt progress.' You will learn what you do not know and continually renew the sense of that poverty.

In the last analysis, the principle or source of the difference between the two languages or discourses is what they lack, what is unexpressed in verbal and non-verbal languages which must perpetually signify that which separates and unites us: the not (perhaps not yet) said. However, there is an ever present temptation. We can infer what that is from Maimonides' instruction. As a desert ascetic implied even longer ago, it is the temptation not to recognize our poverty and so to identify ourselves and others with some satisfaction or assurance. It is agreeing and expecting others to agree to be and do what is merely 'expected' or certain. It is stopping there merely to repeat the past.

What one wants to do

What one wants depends less upon what has been said than upon what may yet be seen. As Certeau once said, 'Seeing is more important.' This is as true today for a Christian as for any scientist. Verification is about what can be truly expressed. Authentic scientists find the basis for verification of their theories in observable phenomena. Likewise, what matters more globally is less what is not said and more what is actually seen.

That certainly means that, returning to themselves, Christians seek to offer observable evidence of their belief or love. Because that is a human endeavour, it is a religious endeavour. As suggested previously, for those who say they are

The Wisdom of Uncertainty

Christians there is a call to witness their faith and charity. As John's Jesus says, 'others will know you are my disciples by your love'. For the Christian at least, the conversion of the hypothetical conclusion, 'God exists', to visible fact is when and to the extent that the prediction born of the hypothesis is exemplified. That God exists is seen as fact when Christians act in accord with Jesus' command: Love your enemies. That is, by the extent to which Christians try to identify neither themselves nor others with any expected satisfactions or assurances, others know who Christians enigmatically re-present: the other/Other – the Surprising Stranger, the Misunderstood Unknown, the Thief.

In the final analysis, what Thérèse de Liesiux's remark – 'I believe because I want to' – tells us is not what she wants but rather Whom she wants. The way of the Pilgrim is the way of the wisdom of uncertainty, of belief in others funded by the poverty underlying her confession.

Questions

What makes two different but parallel discourses or languages necessary?

Why do I think the Pilgrim says that it is an illusion to think that 'what one says is no different from what one is speaking of?' Do I know this from my own experience?

Why is poetry so important when it comes to the dialogue of philosophy and theology?

In the Pilgrim's view, what must a visitor bring to *The Stranger* so that it is no more than a dead letter?

What is it about the Pilgrim's description of the mystic which makes them so ordinary and unexceptional? What makes a mystic Christian?

Notes

1. *L'Absent de l'histoire*, pp. 54–68.
2. Genesis 32:23–32.
3. Job 40:4.
4. Certeau, 'Mystique' ('Mysticism'), France, *Encyclopedia Universalis*, 2007.
5. Certeau, 'Mystique'.
6. See *The Confessions of St. Augustine*, Book Nine.
7. Certeau, *La Fable Mystique*, 411.
8. Certeau, *Il Parlare Angelico, Figure per una poetica della Lingua (Secoli XVI–XVII)*, 'Lo spazio del desiderio, gli "Ezercizi Spirituali" di Loyola.' Florence, Italy: Leo S. Olschki, 1988, 109.
9. Certeau, *La Fable Mystique*, p. 411.

Chapter 6

Whither Has Our Guide Brought Us?

Words still go out softly towards the unsayable.
Rainer Maria Rilke

The Pilgrim has made it possible for us to see four things. We have methodically analysed a brief text regarding human faith or trust. We have come to understand trust in the Other, God, through better understanding our human trust in others, recognizing its beginning and ending in the unknown. That is, as a believer, I am a human who, to the extent that one can, recognizes the limits of their ability to grasp others (and the Other) and in words and deeds seeks the sense of that recognition, union in difference.

We have seen how our Guide opens to us a theoretical understanding of spirituality based upon asking how one understands humanity, others and the Other. We have seen how the Pilgrim suggests to us a way of proceeding in relation to others and the Other based upon the confession of our incapacity to know them. In other words he has given us some insight into what I call a way of the 'wisdom of uncertainty'.

Ithaca

Ithaca is where Odysseus, Ionian Homer's hero, returns at the climax of his eventful voyage back from war. Ithaca means home. For us the Pilgrim's dual paragraph is an Ithaca-home, a place from which one begins and to which one returns.

One can't go home again in the sense that neither the homeplace nor the one who returns are the same as before their separation. And that is the point: both the Pilgrim's paragraph and we ourselves are changed by our having thought about belief and faith. Recognizing, to the extent that we can, the limits of our ability to grasp others and the Other, we become believers in others and perhaps even faithful.

Ithaca stands for anything without which we could not exist. As Constantine P. Cavafy, a twentieth-century Greek poet in Alexandria, Egypt, concludes his poem 'Ithaca' (1911):

> Ithaca has given you the beautiful voyage
> Without her you would never have taken the road
> But she has nothing more to give you.
> And if you find her poor, Ithaca has not defrauded you.
> With the great wisdom you have gained, with so much
>   experience,
> You must surely have understood by then what Ithacas mean.

I believe the dual paragraph has more to give us; it is not spent. If one feels defrauded, it is due not to the Pilgrim's text but to our inability to adequately assay the rich veins it contains. On the other hand, if in it we spy something crystalline or golden, that is, if we discover something worth our investment, then in the words of another twentieth-century poet, T. S. Eliot in 'Little Gidding' (1942):

> We shall not cease from exploration
> And the end of all our exploring
> Will be to arrive where we started
> And know the place for the first time.

Exploration begins and ends with the unknown.

'One of the boldest ... and most sensitive minds of our time ... '

We conclude with reflections upon some words from the beginning of chapter one, words of the Bulgarian-born feminist, philosopher and analyst Julia Kristeva. To the extent that the preceding study has fairly 'decoded' Certeau's paragraph, disclosed the thinking of its author, then we have at least glimpsed the boldness and sensitivity of the person from whom it comes.

Certeau's sensitivity is that of someone always in charge of himself, always a sincere partner in dialogue, modest in his generous care, and ecumenical in his passion. A sensitive partner in dialogue, the Pilgrim practiced to a high degree the initial confession of which he writes. He invites his interlocutors to learn with, rather than from, him.

Someone who is modest in his care, the Pilgrim sincerely practices what he invites us to confess. His is a practice of modesty born of a clear recognition of what he knows he does not know. He gives the words of Abba Joseph, of Maimonides and of many others their contemporary sense. Thus his caring, helping others to grow, is not that of someone wielding power but that of a learned companion on a voyage of discovery. Even if he has many times seen ports we ourselves are only seeing for the first time, he accepts that he, as well as we, may yet find something surprising. He is generous with his company.

Behind his ecumenical or global range of interests and concern, behind his modesty and generosity there is a passion. You may have sensed it while reading the text we have studied. He describes such passion as a necessity and desire to enter history, an altering and altered passion, even a 'rage to love'.[1]

The Pilgrim's boldness comes in his clear articulation of an ordinary challenge to everyone, and especially to one in authority – parents, teachers, missionaries and leaders of every kind, without exception. It is a call to humbly examine every attitude and value in the light of the initial confession of the dual paragraph. In regard to every practical problem, Certeau asks: Do you recognize the unknown? And then, he asks: Since so much is unknown about existence, what way ahead is there, other than to seek the unknown in union with resistant, different others? Can we try to do any more or less than believe in or love one another?

The Pilgrim boldly challenges his interlocutors to continually differentiate themselves – their own thinking and questioning – and to assume their own liberty before the Unknown. He challenges us to respect a similar altered position in any stranger for whom one may have particular responsibility: a child, a spouse, a friend, a co-worker, a co-religionist, any other who takes a position different from one's own in regard to understanding faith or living in a particular group or orienting oneself toward others.

Thus, Certeau gives us a contemporary understanding of that fundamental presupposition of Ignatius of Loyola: that it is necessary for partners in dialogue always to be more ready to put a good construction upon an other's words rather than to condemn them as false; more ready to question and learn than to avoid or eliminate. That is, partners in dialogue are ever disposed to identify neither themselves nor others with any satisfactions or assurances they might wish to gain from or to impose upon an other. That is what 'indifference' or 'detachment' are meant to refer to. It is a norm for discernment, a guideline whenever I examine why I want what I want.

'One of the most secret minds of our time ...'

We come to the question of a secret of the Pilgrim's mind: Can we say that we have found one? Perhaps so – at least to the extent that we have shown that what is called his 'way of standing in the question' is surely rooted in his persistent recognition of poverty and the structure of belief. Probably not so, for it should be evident that we must recognize in him the unknown; that this significant by-passer ever remains a stranger, beyond our grasp. Furthermore, as the Austrian philosopher at Cambridge University Ludwig Wittgenstein said, 'That whereof we cannot speak we must consign to silence.'

On the other hand, nothing prevents resisting even Wittgenstein and, while confessing our ignorance, asking the question from a different point of view. It was said by St Athanasius that God became human that humans might become God, likenesses of the divine. In that sense, is Certeau a saint?

Though I have my opinion, I alone would never publicly ask this. Furthermore, at the beginning of his *Mystic Fable*, the Pilgrim writes modestly that he 'would wish to avoid ... the "prestige" ... of having [his writing] taken as a discourse accredited by a presence, authorized to speak in its name; that is, supposed to know that whereof it speaks'.[2]

Nonetheless, the Pilgrim's biographer, François Dosse, reports the discrete observations of two people who encountered Certeau in their own lives. It is through them that the biographer makes the question public. They speak of what I would describe as a 'certain' quiet, reserved, yet open and caring attractiveness. One speaks of how Certeau seemed to have a deep personal knowledge of him and of how this experience provoked him to wonder about the Pilgrim's sanctity. Another, who happens to be a Jew, testifies that there is 'something of that kind' about him. To them at least it seemed he was a living icon, like the sacred images of Greek Orthodox Christians. As Leonide Ouspensky explains, what is important about an icon or holy image is what it has in common with its prototype, with Christ or a saint. An icon represents another's participation in the divine life.[3] That is the sense to which Athanasius was pointing. Is the Pilgrim a participant, a likeness expressive of that sense, a significant union in difference? Given what I have attempted to show about the elegance of the Pilgrim's thinking and given the fulfilment of the biblical rule about the possible truth of a proposition requiring two witnesses, I say: We can ask that.

Notes

1. Certeau, *Le Cristianisme éclaté*, pp. 91–2.
2. Certeau, *La Fable Mystique*, p. 9.
3. Ouspenky, Leonide, *Theology of the Icon*, Crestwood, New York, St Vladimir's Seminary Press, 1978.

Bibliographic notes on *L'étranger ou l'union dans la différence*

To the extent that my marginal remarks on a few words of the Pilgrim have sparked the reader's interest in knowing more about Certeau, much of his work is available in translation. It is easily found by doing a search on Michel de Certeau on the internet. Below I give a list in French of his longer works, many of which are in translation.

The Pilgrim's French text of *L'étranger* has appeared in three editions. The first served as the principal basis for this study. It appeared in 1969 through the publisher Desclée de Brouwer as part of a line entitled '*Foi Vivante*' (Living Faith). One may occasionally find a copy of it through sellers online, for example abebooks.com. The text awaits an English translation.

The first edition is especially interesting because it contains all the notes supplied by Certeau. They document the depth and breadth of his reading. They are also interesting for the suggestive questions and quotations which they contain. Those were posed nearly forty years ago but they still remain pertinent. Here is an example for students of the past (it has psychological implications as well): 'How [are we] to situate the difference of a past in relation to a present, or of a present in relation to a past, so that one admits the other and so that one is not contrary to the other?' In other words, he is asking: Isn't it the goal of the historian to represent the past in such a way that we see not only its difference from but also its union with the (changing) present? At the same time, does it not make sense to say that the goal of psychological development is to recognize ever more fully the union and difference of one's past and present?

Many more questions from the Pilgrim's notes in *L'étranger* could be added, but the foregoing suggest well enough the many faceted complexity of the Pilgrim's thought. They suggest one more thing: how conversant the Pilgrim was with thinkers of his own day. He took them seriously, questioned them, learned from them and in the process differentiated himself from them.

A second edition of *L'étranger* appeared in 1991, again through Desclée de Brouwer. This edition differs from the first in five ways, none of which harm the integrity of the Pilgrim's thought. It incorporates corrections of the first edition originally made by Certeau himself with fewer notes and the addition of an introductory chapter, written by Certeau himself; however, it lacks his brief foreword to the first edition. It has an introduction by Professor Luce Giard, colleague of Certeau, in charge of his literary estate.

The third edition of *L'étranger* appeared in 2005, its publisher is Éditions du Seuil. This repeats the text of the 1991 edition but is preceded with a new introduction by Professor Giard. It is available from the publisher.

Books by Michel de Certeau

What is included here, with thanks to Professor Luce Giard, are the main works of Michel de Certeau in French. Reference has been made to the complexity of the Pilgrim's thought. In these works, one may find that one wishes his thought were less complex, but the endeavour to comprehend is worth the effort.

For further information about his published works, including those translated into English, one can go to 'the untimely past', (http://www.untimelypast.org/bibcert.html). It thus contains much valuable information. The following list contains several even more recent French editions of his work.

Le Memorial de Pierre Favre, Desclée de Brouwer, 1960.
Guide spirituel de Jean-Joseph Surin, Desclée de Brouwer, 1963.
Correspondance de Jean-Joseph Surin, Desclée de Brouwer, 'Bibliothèque européene', 1966.
La Prise de parole (1968), Repris dans La Prise de parole et autres écrits politiques, Seuil, 'Points Essais' n° 281, 1994.
La Possession de Loudon (1970), nouv. ed., Gallimard, 'Folio Histoire', 2005.
L' Absent de l'histoire, Mame, 1973.
Le Christianisme éclaté, (en collaboration avec Jean-Marie Domenach), Seuil, 1974.
La Culture au pluriel (1974). nouv. éd., Seuil, 'Points Essais' n° 267.1993.

L'Écriture de l'istoire (1975), Gallimard, 'Folio Histoire', 2002.

Une politique de la langue La révolution française et les patois: La enquete de Gregoire (1975), (En collaboration avec Dominique Julia et Jacques Revel), nouv. éd., Gallimard, 'Folio Histoire', 2002.

L'Invention du quotidien, t.1 Arts de faire (1980). nouv. éd., Gallimard, 'Folio Essais',1990.

'Invention du quotidien, 1. 2 Habiter, cuisiner (1980). (en collaboration avec Luce Giard et Pierre Mayol), nouv. éd., Gallimard, 'Folio Essais',1994.

La Fable mystique XVI-XVIJ siecle t. 1 (1981), 2 éd., Gallimard, 'Tel', 1987.

L'Ordinaire de la communication, (en collaboration avec Luce Giard), Dalloz, 1983.

Histoire et psychanalyse entre science et fiction (1987) nouv. ed., Gallimard, 'Folio Histoire', 2002.

La Faiblesse de croire (1987), 2 éd, Seuil, 'Points Essais', n. 504, 2003.

Le Lieu de l'autre, Gallimard-Seuil, 'Hautes Etudes', 2005.

www.ingramcontent.com/pod-product-compliance
Lightning Source LLC
Chambersburg PA
CBHW032302150426
43195CB00008BA/543